"Rob Wrubel has written another must-read for anyone who has a family member or friend with special needs. It is clear that he has a deep passion for helping families with special-needs members get and stay on track financially. His personal commitment is not only inspiring, it's infectious. Read this book — and learn from one of the best."

> **– Jack Canfield**, Co-Author of *The Success Principles™* and *Chicken Soup for the Soul®*

"As parents of a special needs child, my wife and I are always sensitive to whatever valuable information is out there in the ongoing pursuit of providing the best possible life-long care and comfort for our child. Rob Wrubel's book is an important tool in that arsenal of vital information."

> **– Joe Mantegna**, Tony Award-winning Actor nominated for multiple Grammy and Golden Globe Awards

"Rob Wrubel draws on his personal and professional experience to enable all families, and especially those confronted with disability, to ensure a more secure future."

> **– David Hirsch**, Founder of 21st Century Dads Foundation, author and host of the Special Fathers Network Dad to Dad Podcast

"Rob Wrubel has created a fantastic tool in *30 Days to Your Special Needs Trust* that will inform and motivate people who have been struggling to complete their estate plans. The book will motivate readers to make decisions and get their plan in place, recognizing that perfection is the enemy of progress."

– **Steve Ogle**, Estate Planning Attorney

"As an estate planning attorney who practices in the area of special needs, this book will be a go-to reference source for my clients to better understand and navigate a very important and complex aspect of their lives."

– **Spencer Gresham**, Estate Planning Attorney

"Rob Wrubel continues in his tradition of making a complicated and sometimes stressful topic manageable for families with special needs children in his third book. His stories and examples are illustrative and bring the reader through the chapters, following up each topic with helpful worksheets at the end of the book. As a special-needs estate planning attorney, I couldn't ask for a better homework assignment for all my clients!"

– **Annette Hines**, Attorney, special needs mom and author of *Butterflies and Second Chances*, and host of Parenting Impossible: The Special Needs Survival Podcast

30 Days to Your

SPECIAL NEEDS TRUST

A Quick-Start Guide to Your Special-Needs Estate Plan

ROB WRUBEL, CFP®

Published by Rosalibean Publishing, LLC

ISBN 978-0-9966592-3-9 (paperback)
ISBN 978-0-9966592-4-6 (e-book)

Printed in the United States of America

CONTENTS

30 Days to Your

SPECIAL
NEEDS
TRUST

FOREWORD

I am lucky – my world grows fuller and richer as I get to meet so many people who thrive and stay strong when it seems like life is stacked against them. I can point to several ways my life is better for meeting people with developmental disabilities and I hope that I have offered enough kindness and joy to help as well.

Families have let me into their hearts at all different times – in hospital rooms, football games, in their homes and out at restaurants, stores and parades. I cannot imagine my life without meeting strong, funny and wonderful people with differing abilities.

Today, we live in a moment when inclusion and fairness are on the rise and I love seeing the faces and hearing the stories of people gaining access in our communities. I grew up in a time when people with developmental differences were not seen, they were not part of my daily life and I never thought too much about that. Fortunately, that has changed for the better.

When Rob asked me to write a foreword to this book, he asked me a few questions about why I am active in meeting people with developmental disabilities and acting as a spokesperson for events and organizations like Special Olympics. He asked, "Why do I give so much to others and why do I keep doing it?"

I never thought about it too much – I love meeting people and it lifts me up when I help others as we share a moment of laughter and connection. I feel really good when I connect with others and the more that happens the more I want to do. I recommend it – especially if you are feeling down about yourself. Don't take my word for it, try it out. Even something small helps – return a grocery cart for a stranger the next time you are at a store or find some other small way to help and you will see how good it feels. Stepping up to help even one person leads to amazing healing in your own life and can take your life in all kinds of positive directions.

A funny thing happened when I became well-known. It started when I first appeared on TV and then as soon as Modern Family aired and became a hit TV show, the quantity of people in my life jumped. I was asked to say hello to people including those in hospitals and bring some compassion, fun and entertainment to people going through tough times.

One of my most memorable visits was with a boy in his hospital room about four years ago. I was nervous about how I could interact with this young man. He was non-verbal and I did not fully understand his disability at the time. I was in my own space thinking about how I could connect.

When I walked into the room, his Dad lit up with a big smile. That sure helped. The boy had a tablet on his lap and he was listening to Sia's song "Chandelier." Well, I just started singing along with the song, "I'm gonna swing from the chandelier..." and dancing to the music. In an instant, we connected and had a great time. The boy had a huge grin as we shared a touching and heartfelt time.

I left the room feeling like I had won the lottery – my quick visit lead to a big moment for the family when they were facing tough times and a huge one for me. I left the room zapped, excited and feeling like I had done some good.

This one moment just kept giving, to me and to the family as I have had the chance to see them several times and hear more about their journey.

The nurse in that room tweeted nice thoughts about that day and as I headed back to Los Angeles we stayed in touch. And we kept staying in touch. And finally, we got to see each other again in the real world. Today, I am still with that nurse and Lindsay is the love of my life.

As I think more about the wonderful people I now know, I also keep coming back to how amazing so many people with developmental disabilities act in social situations, and how we all would be better by being open to more inclusion and interactions. I feel like I want to bottle whatever it is in a person with a developmental disability that leads them to smile at the person nearest to them or to try to start a conversation in a store or restaurant. Sure, there is that moment of awkwardness – how often does someone start a conversation when standing in line at a store or sitting down in a restaurant? Not nearly often enough. When it happens, our lives become brighter for that moment.

I help people and causes where I am truly passionate. Each year, I am impressed and amazed by the parents of a family member with an intellectual or developmental disability. They work so hard to open doors for their family members and enjoy each day as a new and exciting adventure.

Schools, social media, people talking to each other. We have so many ways today to meet and interact with the people around us. I know we have work to do to include everyone in these interactions. I also know how important it is to reach out, raise awareness and acknowledge the gifts each person brings. I am so lucky to have been able to meet and be a part of the journey of so many people with developmental disabilities and their families.

The book in your hands encourages you to take an important planning step to protect benefits that your family member most likely will need. Rob and I talked about his work and his family, and I know he has a big heart as he seeks to educate families like his. I hope this book will help you as you plan for the future.

— **Eric Stonestreet**, Emmy award-winning actor

INTRODUCTION

My house was built in 1904. It's a Craftsman style dwelling with open rooms and geometric woodwork and the house has a warm, inviting, and welcoming feel. I've heard from neighbors that the original owners most likely bought a design kit from Sears or another provider, hired a builder, and customized the basic design to fit their vision of the home. There's another house in my neighborhood from the same kit with just enough differences to make them both unique and personal.

Like any older home, it's needed updating—and it seems like every owner has done something to improve the house and bring it into the modern world. The kitchen was remodeled decades ago; eventually I, too, will remodel the kitchen. Last year, I installed new ovens, which meant updating the utility service, changing the circuit-breaker panel, and installing new wiring to the kitchen appliances.

On top of that, I've removed wallpaper in several rooms and brought a modern paint scheme into parts of the house. The floors were redone at least once and maybe more. Plumbing fixtures are so different now than they were more than a hundred years ago, and I've replaced most of them with modern ones in the eight years since I've owned the home.

The home meets our needs, and it's been a great place to raise my family. I expect to live here for many years, and don't have any desire to move. That could change even if I don't expect it to. The elderly person before me installed bars at the stairways and in the bathrooms, which extended her stay in the home, although eventually she had to move as her health declined. That could be me decades from now. There are other reasons that could necessitate a move—finances, health, a better location, or the need for different kinds of rooms or more space.

As I wrote this book, I kept thinking about the similarities between my old house and estate planning for families with special-needs members.

While no one wants to renovate or upgrade a house, people feel called upon to make changes to their abodes to live more comfortably, safely, and with greater enjoyment. In my house, that old paint worked fine, and the color wasn't awful. It just wasn't as interesting and cheerful as the new paint.

The time and investment you spend on a home can increase your financial, emotional, and psychological well-being. To make changes, you have to take action, be uncomfortable for a fixed period of time, and put yourself in the hands of capable professionals.

It's not much different with estate planning. While no one wants to visit an attorney and draft or update an estate plan, doing so can help you live more comfortably, safely, and with increased enjoyment.

I hear people express fear when they explain why they have not put an estate plan in place. They worry about high costs, facing too many decisions, and making mistakes. I get it, and every time I think about a home project, the similarities between home projects and estate planning is clear.

Estate planning with special-needs considerations requires the help of experts. They speak a different language, one we don't often understand. They understand how crucial decisions work together to achieve desired outcomes.

I've never wanted to design and build a new home; I much prefer choosing from what's available. It would take me years to design my own home and decades to build one—and in the meantime, it could come crashing to the ground.

Recently, I replaced an oven. Not too hard, right? I wish. My home is older, and there was not a simple way to buy a new oven that would fit in the old cabinets. I needed help, and so I hired a cabinet-specialist friend to make recommendations and oversee the process. It cost less than I expected, and it transformed my kitchen.

Take this same approach with your estate plan and use this book to simplify the process. Find an expert in special-needs trusts in your area. Gain some basic knowledge of the purpose of these trusts and on how they fit into your long-range financial and life plans. Make the important decisions and let the experts design and finalize the work.

Blueprints

My Blueprints method utilizes the house as a metaphor for special-needs planning. No one buys or builds a house without first envisioning where they'll live, deciding what style of house they want, and having some kind of plan in place. New homes require an architect who pulls together the dreams and desires of the client and who maps those out in detailed drawings.

The special-needs trust is the foundation of the overall plan—you don't want to amass investments and assets only to have them wasted as a result of poor estate planning. The trust ensures that family resources are used to improve each family member's quality of life and not spent on basics already covered by benefits.

Good estate planning puts your wishes in writing. A good plan lets you choose where your money goes, who steps in to help you and your family, and how you manage your taxes. Without a good plan, you are at the mercy of the courts, your family, and the state rules governing social programs. Don't leave these major decisions to chance. Give your family direction. Protect benefits and the environment you've put in place for your son or daughter with a developmental disability. And do it soon.

Through my work, I regularly meet and interact with attorneys. I consult with people both prior to their engaging an attorney and after they have put estate plans in place, and I've read many wills and trusts. Each year, I spend hours in professional education, increasing my understanding of estate planning, and I'm an accredited estate-planning professional with the National Academy of Estate Planners (NAEPC). I've used this experience to simplify the steps most people need to take in deciding how to best serve their loved ones.

You can have your estate plan in place in the next thirty days. Use the worksheets in each chapter, put the right names with the jobs that need to be done, and set up a meeting with a qualified attorney in your state. You'll feel better once you've taken this giant step, knowing you can turn your focus to the other building blocks of special-needs planning.

Using This Book

At its most basic level, an estate plan tells your family, friends, creditors, and governments who gets your assets when you die, who gets to distribute those assets, and who gets to make medical and financial decisions if you're still alive but incapacitated. For countless reasons, estate planning can be complex, as estates can include planning for multiple generations, tax efficiency, legacy gifts to charities, and the handling of sophisticated business interests.

But don't let this level of complexity get in the way of making the simple decisions quickly. The core of planning for most people means assigning the right people to the right roles. In this book, you will learn the following words, what they mean, and the types of people suited to carry out certain responsibilities for you: *beneficiary*, *trustee*, *guardian*, *personal representative*, and *powers of attorney*.

My feeling is that once you've identified those people you wish to fill these roles, or once you know you don't have anyone in your life who can fill these roles, you can get moving. A good attorney will guide you through the process, review the people you've selected, and then add other estate techniques, if needed, for your family. Approach this work with an open mind—it's possible you have it all mapped out and just need the attorney to draft your documents. It's equally possible that the attorney's expertise will present you with new options that will create even better outcomes.

Many of the chapters in this book have worksheets or checklists to help you. Use them. Write down names, dates, and any questions that jump to mind. Go with your gut instincts. Listen to your heart.

You are trying to put plans in place to take care of your family member who needs support. You will feel so much better when your estate plan is done. Let's get started, and good luck.

Follow these guidelines when using this book:

1. Finish each exercise. Using the worksheets or a notebook, capture your thoughts as they come.

2. Let your heart guide you. You can spend hours on each chapter, running countless scenarios for each decision, but at some point you need to make a choice. If you cannot decide, write down several names and discuss them with your professional team. It's likely you know the right answer in your heart but allow other factors get in your way.

3. Perfection is not your goal. Nobody can replace you as parent, mentor, coach, and family leader. You will need to name people to fill some of these roles and hope they do their best if called.

4. Don't censor yourself. Write down one name or ten names on each worksheet. Write as many as you can on the first try. Prioritize them at a later time or under the guidance of your attorney and professional team.

5. Don't delay. You have this book; use it. The legal work you need to do is a critical part of making life the best it can be for your entire family. Waiting increases stress and takes away your enjoyment of each day.

PART 1

THIRTY DAYS TO YOUR SPECIAL-NEEDS TRUST

CHAPTER 1

WHAT'S HOLDING YOU BACK?

Jane, age eighty, lives with her fifty-five-year-old daughter Stella. Jane lives on Social Security and her deceased husband's pension, and yet she still saves money each month. She owns her home, is free of debt, and spends less than she earns.

Jane scrimped and saved her entire life. She grew up and raised her children in an era when people did not expect to use governmental benefits, and she does her best to care for herself and family. She lives modestly, drives an old car, and her house needs some work. Jane's health is okay, though she has slowed down during the last three years; she may need long-term care support in the next decade.

Her family never earned more than average, yet she's managed to build her savings and retirement accounts; she has close to $250,000 in assets in addition to her house. She's never felt wealthy even though she knows she has enough money to last the rest of her life.

Stella has intellectual and developmental disabilities. She worked part-time in sheltered employment for thirty years until the organization she worked for closed their facility. Stella goes to day programs four days per week hosted by two different nonprofits. Supplemental Security Income (SSI) pays for Stella's expenses, and she receives state-funded supports that cover the cost of the day programs, and she is on a waiting list in her state for comprehensive benefits that will help if Jane passes away or can no longer live at home.

There's one big problem: Jane's estate plan leaves her house and her retirement, bank, and investment accounts to Stella. Jane figures that $250,000 will be enough for Stella to live comfortably for the rest of her life. But Jane has not calculated the true value of Stella's benefits, and she has not thought about all the things she provides to Stella that benefits do not cover.

Stella's health insurance comes from Medicaid-funded services, as does her day program. If Stella continues to live at home, the supports she needs will be provided by a nonprofit agency that receives funds from Medicaid. Her income comes from the SSI benefit program. In this book, I'll show you a quick calculation that demonstrates how these benefits can be worth millions of dollars.

These benefits will be lost if Jane does not plan correctly. If Stella has more than $2,000 in her name, she will lose those benefits—and given the size of Jane's estate, she will have far more than $2,000. By taking one simple planning step, Jane can protect that money, protect Stella's benefits, and use the money to improve Stella's quality of life. Jane can include provisions in her estate plan for a special-needs trust.

The special-needs trust is a vehicle allowed by law to hold investments and assets that can benefit Stella without eliminating her from her benefit programs. These trusts, sometimes referred to as *supplemental-needs trusts*, are a critical planning tool for families with a member who has an intellectual or developmental disability.

This book is designed to encourage you to get your estate plan with special-needs provisions in place and get it done quickly.

Like many people in her situation, Jane spends her time caring for her family member with a disability. Her days and weeks are filled with Stella's needs; it's busy, stressful, and immediate. She rarely takes time for herself, and the last thing she wants to do is gaze into the future and worry about her own demise, who will take care of her daughter, and who can step into her shoes as Mom.

Jane needs to act. No one can replace her as Mom, but others will have to replace Jane in her many other roles. Someone will have to help Stella eat, take care of her living space, and buy her clothes. Someone will have to get her to doctor and therapy appointments and make sure she takes her medications. She'll also need someone to help her with getting to social opportunities through her day programs and making sure her utility, phone, and television providers are paid.

The special-needs trust helps maintain benefit programs that enable nonprofits to care for a family member with a qualifying disability. Even more than that, the trust can provide a source of funds that improves the quality of life above and beyond what those programs pay for.

What's Holding You Back?

Whenever I speak at workshops and conferences around the country, I always ask the same two questions: "How many of you have heard of special-needs trusts?" and "How many of you have your special-needs trust in place?" In most cases, about 50 percent of families have heard of these trusts, though that number has increased since I first started asking.

Unfortunately, responses also show that fewer than 20 percent of families have done anything to make special-needs provisions part of their estate plan. That number has *not* changed since I started asking. And that number is way too low, leaving too many adults with disabilities at risk. This poll speaks to the fact that people need a quick, simple strategy they can use to take steps to protect benefits.

Why is this number so low? Where are you in that poll?

From what I can tell, there are a few reasons people don't move forward:

Cost. People think estate plans are expensive.

Confusion. Most of us don't understand wills, trusts, and legal documents and how it all fits together, which prevents us from hiring the professionals who do understand it.

Fear. We fear making mistakes. We fear what we don't understand and feel intimidated by the process. We also fear the future, and taking the time to plan for it can be painful, upsetting, and, therefore, easy to push off for another day.

Lack of knowledge. Most people don't know even the basics when it comes to starting a will and estate plan, and they don't want to go to a lawyer without being more educated.

Time constraints. Other activities call for our time. Many of these are enjoyable, and we'd rather spend time doing something we love than puzzling through a document that reminds us of our mortality.

Do you know what's holding you back? In talking with attorneys and families, I find that once the key decisions are made, it's pretty easy to get wills and trusts finalized. This book will help you make those key decisions.

Your Special-Needs Trust

A special-needs trust isn't like winning the lottery—you don't get a huge cash infusion that solves your financial concerns forever. Unlike the lottery, you *can* win the special-needs sweepstakes every time: it's not a game of chance. Good estate planning protects family assets and preserves benefits—benefits, as you will read in the next chapter, that can be worth millions of dollars. And it's a jackpot you know you will win.

Families like ours gain more than financial benefits by putting estate plans in place; we gain a degree of comfort knowing that funding is available to pay for food and shelter for our family member with a disability. Unlike other parents, we assume that it's unlikely our family member will live independently or live outside the home without support. A funded special-needs trust does not guarantee that our loved one with special needs lives a fulfilling life, but it does protect benefits that can provide essentials while making resources available to be spent to maintain the quality of life we expect for our family members.

This book is for people who have heard of the concept of the special-needs trust but who, for whatever reason, haven't moved ahead with getting an estate plan with a trust in place. It's written to encourage you to move forward and move quickly. Benefits are too valuable to risk waiting. Why not get started on these key planning tasks so you can focus on enjoying and appreciating each day instead of stressing about the future?

CHAPTER 2

THE VALUE OF BENEFITS

"See a penny, pick it up, and all day long you'll have good luck." We all know that little rhyme, and now, thanks to me, you will have it stuck in your head for the rest of the day. We could all use a little good luck in our lives, and if it's as simple as stopping every so often to pick up a penny, why not do it?

Pennies are funny things in today's world of e-commerce, credit cards, and click-of-a-button purchases. Pennies are small, solid, and of little value for shopping. Yet, we love them.

There are a few funny things about pennies that are good to know.

In 2019, the penny cost the US Mint 1.99 cents to make each one. That's not a great investment, but every time the government talks about phasing out the penny, public backlash keeps it in circulation. There's an entire school of economics explaining that we do not always make rational choices. Nothing shows that to be truer than spending two cents to get one.

Our "copper" penny is actually copper-plated zinc.

Abraham Lincoln was the first president to be featured on any coin when he was honored on the one-hundredth anniversary of his birthday in 1909. President Theodore Roosevelt had asked for the penny and other coins to be redesigned, as he thought they lacked artistic merit.

Even though our little rhyme tells us we will have good luck by picking up that penny, the financial incentive to pick it up is just not there. The federal minimum wage is $7.25 an hour. That means you'd have to pick up 725 pennies every hour, or one penny every 12 seconds, just to earn minimum wage. Many states have even higher minimum wages, which means that taking the time to search for those pennies and pick them up is a losing game. A person is far better off working, right?

There's an interesting bit of math if you do take pennies from your income and save them. Here's what happens if you take one penny every day and add it to your pennies from the previous day: On day one, save one penny. On day two, add two pennies to the first so you have three pennies. Keep doing the same thing, and on day three you will have six pennies (1 + 2 + 3 = 6). In a year, you will have $667.95. In two years, $2,668.15. That really proves the old phrase "take care of the pennies and the pounds will take care of themselves." (Of course, if you can do that with dollars, you will really be making financial headway!)

We love our pennies. I rarely spend mine or turn them into dollars. I like having them around, even if they don't add a tremendous amount of financial value to my family's accounts.

Pennies teach us valuable lessons. The simple math exercise above shows how saving pennies can lead to real cash. The fact that we spend twice their value to make them helps us understand that not all decisions are rational.

In special-needs planning, families cannot afford to throw out the simple steps that can lead to preserving significant funds. These "penny ideas" can preserve thousands—or even as much as millions—of dollars in benefits.

Luckily, there is a special-needs planning technique that lets you spend a relatively small amount of money to create significant financial value for your family. In just thirty days, you can move forward with this technique that can help you protect benefits that could be worth tens of thousands, hundreds of thousands, or even millions of dollars.

Really? A Million Dollars?

Once you understand the value of benefit programs, you will want to act quickly to put in place the one strategy that can protect your loved one's valuable benefits.

Adults with qualifying disabilities are supported by several governmental benefit programs. *Supplemental Security Income* (SSI) is an income benefit paid monthly by the Social Security Administration to qualifying adults. *Medicaid*, an umbrella term for combined federal and state programs, supports qualified adults with disabilities through multiple programs, including health insurance, community volunteer opportunities, work supports, and access to food and shelter (these programs differ by state). A quick look at some of these programs shows how valuable they can be to your family member with a qualifying disability.

The first benefit, and frankly the easiest to understand, is SSI. Currently, in 2020, SSI pays an individual up to $783 per month (and some states add to that benefit); expressed a different way, $783 per month equals $9,396 in annual income. Every ten years that a person receives SSI equals $93,960 in income benefits. If your family member gets that benefit at age eighteen and lives to age fifty-eight, she will receive $375,840 dollars in SSI payments over her lifetime. That doesn't even include the fact that this payment goes up with inflation every year.

That's a big number. It's not yet more than $1 million. But wait—there's more.

The next set of benefits comes from Medicaid. Medicaid services are a mix of federal- and state-funded programs delivered by each state, so the types of services and amounts paid vary by state. These services might have a different name depending upon where you live; for example, in California, they're called Medi-Cal.

With so many programs offered through Medicaid, it's easy to get lost. There are health insurance, supported living, and day programs. These might not be enough for your family, they might be underfunded, and they might be hard to access, but they are there.

Let's try to keep it simple and start with health insurance.

Medicaid often pays for health insurance for people with intellectual and developmental disabilities. If you buy health insurance for your family either on your own or through work, you know that premiums are high. Americans spent about $10,000 per person on health care in 2015, and that number has risen about 5.6 percent each year. Your payments may be different, but it's safe to assume a person with a qualifying disability spends more than the average person on health care. But even if we use the figure of $10,000 per year, the Medicaid health benefit alone is worth $100,000 every ten years and equals $400,000 in benefits over a forty-year lifetime.

And Medicaid pays for more. In Colorado, people getting residential services and supports receive a service level through an exam process; the rate paid to support that person depends on the needs and severity of the disability. This can range from about $66 to $230 per day. At $148 per day, which is the average, this translates to $54,000 per year in benefit, $540,00 per decade, and more than $2,160,000 over a forty-year period.

SSI and Medicaid-funded programs could be worth close to $3 million to your family member with a disability:

SSI for forty years = $375,840.

Medicaid health insurance = $400,000.

Additional comprehensive services = $2,160,000.

Combined, that's $2,934,840—a huge number equal to $73,396 per year over that time period!

People with developmental disabilities do not have as many opportunities for full employment as those without them and often do not have the financial capacity to live independently, to have health-care coverage, and to earn enough to pay for food, utilities, entertainment, and social opportunities. They rely on benefit programs for the basics, and it's almost impossible for families to replace the value of those benefit programs.

The One Simple Number That Can Undo It All

One simple number used by the Social Security Administration can cause a person with a qualifying disability to not get benefits or lose those benefits in the future.

That number is $2,000.

If your family member has more than $2,000 of countable resources in his name, he will lose his benefits. His life will change. The SSI income benefit will stop. He will no longer have access to a local nonprofit service organization that provides employment, monitors his health, and provides transportation. He is at risk of losing his health insurance. For a married couple, the limit is $3,000.

The amount of $2,000 has not changed in decades. It's never been indexed to inflation or ratcheted up. The government says that if you want SSI and Medicaid, then you cannot have your own funds.

As you plan, you will want to take steps to keep any countable resources out of your family member's name. Bank accounts, investment funds, retirement accounts, and other assets used for investment purposes are countable resources. A home that's lived in by the person with a qualifying disability, a car used by that person, and that person's household goods are not countable. The Social Security Administration's website has more detailed information about what constitutes countable resources.

While you are alive, you will need to monitor accounts for your family member receiving benefits. If your daughter gets an SSI check each month, that money will need to be spent on her behalf or moved to an ABLE account. The same goes for any income earned or gifts received from family members. Many parents set up a representative payee account for the SSI and earned income; make sure you stay on top of spending that money so it doesn't accumulate.

The SSI benefit of $783 per month is not a lot in today's economy. It won't pay for much in the way of an apartment. On average, Americans spend $233 on food monthly. Food and rent will take all that money for most people. It's fairly easy to spend the money as it comes in; you just have to stay on top of it.

The Big Issue

The bigger issue is what happens when you die. It's likely you will have more than $2,000 to pass on to any heirs. Employer benefit plans will often offer life insurance policies for $50,000 or a year's worth of salary. And retirement accounts will have more than $2,000 for people who've been saving for just a few years. Additional money from homes, cars, investment accounts, and life-insurance policies can add up quickly.

Families just getting started and those who've spent a lifetime saving and investing have the same problem: they don't want to leave money to the family member with a disability. Anyone with term life insurance could have an estate worth hundreds of thousands of dollars. If you leave this money to your child, he or she cannot qualify for benefits or will lose those benefits until that inheritance is spent. It doesn't make sense to save for the future only to lose out on benefit programs that might be worth far more than you've saved.

This is where one planning technique can save the day and where you can spend a few pennies (well, a bit more) to preserve benefits worth vast sums of money.

This technique is the special-needs trust.

Families with a member with a qualifying disability are encouraged to put special-needs provisions into their estate plan and to have a special-needs or supplemental-needs trust created either today or through the will. For more on this, read my book, *Financial Freedom for Special-Needs Families*. Hopefully, if you are reading this, you have heard of a special-needs trust and have some idea of its purpose. Even if you don't, you probably understand the need to have a will in place and to make plans for who gets your assets when you pass.

Money and other assets in a properly drafted and funded special-needs trust do not count as resources. Legislation passed in 1993 allows for the creation of these types of trusts and has been a significant planning technique for families like ours.

You can leave $10,000, $100,000, $1,000,000, or more in this kind of trust and your family member keeps getting her benefits. This is a huge win for you and your family. SSI payments keep coming. Medicaid pays for services. And you've created a fund that can be used to provide a high-quality life for your loved one.

Money in the trust can be used for furniture, cell phones, TVs, subscription services, additional therapies or medical devices, vacations, and more. SSI and Medicaid pay almost enough for food and rent, but they don't pay enough for the kinds of services and items that make life worth living. A special-needs trust does.

The Value of Benefits

The math is easy. Benefits add up. The financial value alone should be enough to motivate anyone reading this book. I hope you'll realize that getting your estate plan in place is worth the time and the effort it takes to clear the hurdles of fear, confusion, and cost.

Remember those pennies we talked about earlier? Estate planning might cost $1,000, $10,000, or more, depending on where you live and your family's financial complexity. Even if you pay $2,500 or $5,000, you are spending pennies compared to the value of the benefit. SSI alone is worth $9,396 in 2020. If you die today and don't direct your assets the right way, that benefit could be lost for some time. There aren't many places you can invest money and double (or more) the benefit in just one year.

I cannot think of another planning technique where so much income and benefit can be created from such a low investment. I know we hope the payoff is way down the road—I want to live a long life after putting my estate plan in place—but we have to be ready for the worst even as we expect the best.

Moving Forward

The rest of this book will help you understand certain crucial decisions you must make as you move forward, most of which have to do with the people you select in your documents. A good lawyer will know the language for the technical elements of your documents—such as which state laws apply and how conflicts are resolved—and will use the *heretofore* and *therefore* and *whereas* language as needed (having read many wills, I have to wonder why lawyers don't write in plain English).

You're going to have choices to make, and most of these choices will involve people. Who will receive inheritances from you and in what portions? Who can make medical and financial decisions for you? Who will take care of your family member with special needs? The rest of this book will give you the titles for each of these roles, a sense of what those roles entail, and the worksheets you should bring with you to that first meeting with your lawyer.

Now that you know about the value of government benefits and the need to keep resources out of your family member's name, let's get you jump-started so you can get your estate plan in place in the next thirty days.

CHAPTER 3

GETTING STARTED

Finalizing your estate plan isn't all that difficult. It would be easy to come up with a list of far more onerous, painful, time-consuming, and complicated activities. I like my dentist, but getting a filling with a crown takes as much time and costs about the same as getting a will done, and the dentist causes much more anxiety. An oil change isn't painful, but even there I get an experienced technician to take care of it. Any mistake on my part could ruin my car. I know runners who'll spend hours training for marathons but won't take the time to create their wills. I have other friends who'll drive hours to taste a new craft beer but won't spend a minute calling an attorney.

In terms of effort and time, getting your estate plan settled falls somewhere between arranging for a physical and getting your taxes done. It requires a small amount of prework—asking friends for referrals to an attorney, setting an appointment, and organizing documents for a few hours. Estate planning is not as much fun as tasting a new microbrew, but it's also not as painful as a root canal.

Considering the time and money you spend on an estate plan, the value of the plan is significant.

Yes, setting up and managing a special-needs trust seems complicated. And yes, most people feel a tremendous amount of emotion at the front end of the estate-planning process. On some level, this process causes us to confront our mortality, which in turn raises concerns about what will happen to our family members after we are gone. After all, we are making plans that come to fruition only at our death or incapacitation. That's enough to make anyone pause for at least a few seconds.

But don't let those thoughts stop you. There's too much at stake. Why take a chance on losing out on money, benefit programs, well-being, physical health, and basic comforts?

The prior chapter helped you understand the financial value of putting an estate plan in place. With good planning, benefits worth hundreds of thousands to millions of dollars can be safeguarded. That should be enough to get your attention even if you are uncertain about what to do and even if you feel uncomfortable doing it.

Again, the purpose of this book is to help you finish your estate plan in the next thirty days. It's completely possible. I've seen it happen. There's no reason to stretch out the time it takes; an estate plan requires a few decisions about the people involved, and it's unlikely those will be different six months or a year from now. Think of this step in your special-needs planning as a sprint, not an endurance contest. If you want to hike the Appalachian Trail or run a marathon, you will need to train, and it will take time. On the other hand, if you want to run (or even just fast-walk) a hundred-yard dash, there's no need for additional training. You just have to get up, get outside, and go. Get your estate plan in place the same way: fill out the worksheets provided, make a few calls, and get going.

Commit To a Date

Look at the worksheet titled "Chapter 3: Commitment Dates." It has spaces for two dates.

☑ Worksheet: **Chapter 3: Commitment Dates**

The first is your commitment date. Read this book, take a few days to process the information, then get started. Choose a date to start your sprint. Enter this date on your calendar and get ready to go.

My daughter with Down syndrome runs track at her high school. At races, the athletes know the order of each race at a meet, and they congregate in a holding area next to the track before each event. The athletes are then called to the track to take their places. My daughter runs the shortest sprint race possible, and she, like all the racers, loads into a starting block on the track when called. She crouches down, puts her feet back, raises her head, and waits. The starting official counts to three, the pistol fires, and the athletes run as fast as they can.

You are now in the holding area waiting to start. Finish reading this book, fill out the worksheets, and commit to a starting date. That's the moment you are loaded in the starting blocks waiting to go. When that day arrives, you are off and moving as fast as you can.

Our brains are wired to complete tasks we choose, especially tasks that we have an emotional stake in finishing, and tasks that have a specific completion date. We can ramp up the ability to achieve a goal by taking the following three steps.

Dr. Gail Matthews of Dominican University published research showing that people who commit to a goal in writing, who share that goal with at least one other person, and who find an accountability partner increase their odds of completing that goal.

For married couples, this should be simple. Together, write the date you plan to start on the worksheet, then verbally agree that you will spend the next thirty days finalizing your estate plan. Every week, check in with each other to see what needs to happen.

If you're single, take similar steps. Find a friend and tell them what you are doing. Ask them to act as your accountability partner.

The second blank space asks you to commit to a meeting date with an attorney. Do not fill this in yet; wait until you've finished the book and read through the chapter that gives you pointers on how to select an attorney. Once you set an appointment with an attorney, write the date on the worksheet. The dates will serve as reminders to finish the worksheets before that meeting if you haven't already done so.

Can't Commit?

Are you hesitating at making a commitment? Does the thought of writing down a start date or searching for an attorney bring up feelings of fear, discomfort, concern, or sadness? Let's get these feelings out of your head and onto paper. For some reason, they seem smaller when written down; even if they don't shrink, what you write down will be a handy reminder as you talk with friends, family, or therapists about why you haven't moved forward with your estate plan.

There are many techniques that can help you release any fears you might have. Maybe just reading about them can help. Let's address them rationally.

Let's talk about some of the fears I commonly hear people talk about:

- I'll make a mistake.
- I'm nervous about working with a professional.

- I need to know every detail before I plan my estate.

- I don't have enough experience or understanding.

- I don't know if I can make the financial commitment.

I'll Make a Mistake

Are you worried you will put something into your will or estate plan that cannot be changed, that will cause problems, or that will cause your family member with special needs to be worse off than if you had not done anything? Let's review whether that is accurate or not.

Estate documents *can* be changed. Your will isn't like the Declaration of Independence or the Gettysburg Address; it's not written into history forever. While you are alive, your estate documents can be changed easily. If you have not funded a trust, the trust can also be changed. All it takes is a simple call to your attorney and a few hours of your time.

Changes are usually necessitated by a specific event: A dramatic improvement in your finances could trigger a need to update documents. Laws governing trusts and governmental benefits can prompt a review. As you will see in the next chapters, the most critical decisions you make have to do with people—those people you assign to critical jobs. If someone you choose moves, dies, or has a major life change, you might have to replace them in your estate documents. You can easily change your beneficiaries and the amounts that go to each beneficiary as well as the trustee, POAs, and personal representative.

Mistakes can be corrected—even those that show up after death. While you're alive and before the trust is funded, changes are simple; you just call your attorney and update your documents. After your death, it's still possible to make changes even if the process is more complicated. The biggest mistake is not acting; you leave significant benefits to chance.

You won't review and update your estate documents annually; life doesn't move that fast. Ideally, you should take out your estate documents on a regular basis, maybe every five years, just to see what's there. It's just good to know where your will is stored, if nothing else. If something is wrong or no longer applies when you review your documents, call your attorney and get it fixed.

I'm Nervous about Working with a Professional

It's common for people to be apprehensive about working with a professional. Many people have never hired an attorney, CPA, or financial planner, and they don't know what to expect when walking into the office of one of these professionals. They fear feeling intimidated or stupid or being judged for waiting so long to get the plan started.

Lawyers, CPAs, financial planners, and other professionals have expert knowledge gained from years of study and practice (let's call that *experience*; we hope they're not practicing on you!). Instead of hiring an attorney, CPA or financial planner, you *could* just go online, phone a friend, or "practice" on yourself. It's possible, though unlikely, the results yield a well-written, properly drafted trust, accurate tax return, or successful investment portfolio. But why take a chance when you can rely on the advice and work of the experts?

Most of the professionals I know are caring people who believe that their best work comes in partnership with and in serving their clients. They seek to explain the process, rules, laws, why certain steps are taken, and how their work fits with your other planning. The finest professionals educate their clients about how they work.

Sure, there are lots of stereotypes about tough lawyers; just turn on any evening TV court drama. That's showbiz. My experience is that there are many caring professionals who live to serve you without putting their egos and personalities first.

You can spend twenty minutes online and have a basic understanding of what work will be done; and you can read this book, fill out the worksheets, and be ready to act. That does not mean it will be done right if you do it yourself. What you do might not pass the laws of your state, make the most of your taxes, or protect your family in the long run. A competent professional listens to you because they want to help their clients, and the best ones do that by understanding what outcomes are needed by listening to you, the client.

I Need to Know Every Detail before I Plan My Estate

One father came to my workshop series, dutifully attending each meeting. He took notes, engaged in conversations, and was one of those ideal participants who asked good questions, cheered other people on, and came back each time, ready to learn more. Unfortunately, he missed the main message of my work—take action. He never moved forward with an estate plan.

This person wanted to know every single thing there was to know about a special-needs trust. At first, the questions were helpful for the entire class as they were general in nature: "What can the trust buy?" "How can it be funded?" "I'm thinking of this person to name as trustee—does that make sense?" Those are important questions you will have to answer now or later.

He kept asking questions about small details, like state laws, specific purchases that could or could not be made, how taxes are handled in the trust, and more. These were important questions but irrelevant ones without having set up the trust in the first place. Don't stop your planning just because you don't have every single question answered. There's always more to learn, more experience to gain, and you can update your documents as you go.

Chances are, you will live many years into the future, for years or decades, after putting your special-needs estate plan in place. We do the work now to protect our families in case we experience an unexpected, early death.

If you're the type of person who needs and wants to know more about these trusts and how they work, it's likely you'll have plenty of time to learn all you need after getting one in place. Work with your professional team to initiate the work, and learn as you go. Remember, as long as you don't have funds in the trust, you can change pretty much everything.

I Don't Have Enough Experience or Understanding

My Blueprints workshop series goes through the nine building blocks I talk about in my book, *Financial Freedom for Special-Needs Families*. Eight of my workshop sessions take less than ninety minutes to complete each. Workshop participants engage in specific exercises, and there's plenty of time for questions.

The session addressing special-needs planning and the special-needs trust takes the longest and generates the most questions because workshop attendees often get lost in the details of the trust and forget its main purpose: to protect benefits.

On some level, the concepts of special-needs estate planning are easy to grasp:

- Write a will that directs assets to heirs (beneficiaries).

- In that will, include language that creates a trust for assets that could go to a person with a qualifying disability.

- Direct the share of your assets for your family member with a disability to that trust.

- Name someone to oversee those assets (a trustee).

It's really that simple. Make two or three decisions and let the attorney do the work.

Don't get stuck in the minutiae of how the special-needs trust works, who manages it, what purchases can be made, how it gets invested, and how it gets funded. Those details matter; they just don't matter much if the trust is not set up and, ultimately, funded. Once it's in place, you'll have time to learn about how trusts operate, are taxed, and make distributions.

You don't have to be an expert to have a trust. In the mornings, I open the garage door, get into my car, turn the key in the ignition, and drive to work. Every step of that daily routine requires complex actions, but I don't think about how it all happens. How does the car work? I really don't have any understanding of car mechanics. I do know that I turn the key and that sends a signal to some car part that signals another. Somewhere along the way, the spark plug (do cars still have spark plugs?) ignites gas, and the pressure moves a piston that somehow turns the wheel. Really, I don't have any idea how it all works; it just does, and off I go to the office.

The trust is similar. With the help of a capable professional team, you can learn enough to get moving in the right direction without having to know all the details and mechanics of how each piece fits together. A little bit of knowledge is enough—unless you have lots of time, interest, and energy for estate planning. If you do, maybe law school is in your future.

I Don't Know If I Can Make the Financial Commitment

Money and fear often go hand in hand. Why? The simple penny is just a small piece of metal, the dollar nothing more than a piece of paper with odd coloring and an imprint of our government's idea of art. There's nothing frightening there.

Of course, money is more than a simple piece of paper or stamped metal. We measure success with money. We use it to compare ourselves to others. Many of us feel that if we had more of it, we'd be happier—even though studies show that some people with too much money are miserable.

Most of us agree that there never seems to be enough of it when we really want it, and spending it on a lawyer instead of food, entertainment, a trip, or a new car doesn't exactly spark joy.

An estate plan requires an up-front financial commitment—a genuine hurdle for some, a psychological hurdle for others.

Right now, do you have any idea what you will pay for your estate plan? Probably not. Why not gain a little perspective on what it might cost before you decide the financial commitment is too high or not worth the effort?

The lack of cost clarity works against getting your plan done. The mind races to fill in blanks and often makes bad assumptions. There's an easy fix. Call a few attorneys. Get a range of costs from several of them. Without the perspective of the value you'll be getting, you may worry that the cost is too high. Cost, as investment, yields significant benefits to protect your family member with a disability. Get a cost estimate and compare it to the value of benefits you'll receive.

Some families just don't have money right now. There's no extra savings to spend. If that's you, it's important to commit to a savings timeline and create a way to fund the expense. You will have to take additional steps before hiring an attorney, such as reducing your spending or finding ways to earn more. Can you work extra hours? Can you ask a family member to help? Maybe you can tighten spending in a few areas for a few months to raise enough money. You could stop retirement-plan contributions for a few months. Check with your local bar association to see if they have any estate attorneys willing to volunteer their services.

The financial rewards are clear: the protection of benefits worth irreplaceable sums of money. It's worth getting current cost information on an estate plan and then scrimping to save the funds to get it done. Few investments have the same potential return.

Nelson Mandela has been quoted as saying, "Courage is not the absence of fear, but the triumph over it." Every new task, idea, or activity has some element of risk and the unknown—and some involve a degree of fear. By writing out your fears, taking steps to overcome them, and pushing forward, you will learn a new skill, gain confidence and put a plan in place to protect valuable benefits.

Set things in motion. Write out a date, wait for the starting gun to fire, then get moving as fast as you can so your special-needs trust is in place and you can focus on living an enjoyable and meaningful life.

CHAPTER 4

BENEFICIARIES

Ambrose Bierce is credited with saying, "Death is not the end. There remains the litigation over the estate." By now you are committed to avoiding the major pitfalls that come when you do not have wills and trusts in place. Now, it's time to list the people and organizations that will inherit from you.

The heart of this work is to help others when you can no longer do so. While you are alive, you use your investments and assets to support yourself and to pay for certain expenses for your family member with a qualifying disability. Benefit programs like SSI and Medicaid do not pay enough for the basics, let alone enough to pay for a high quality of life and it's likely you supplement those benefits with income from your own resources to make life enjoyable. You might also be helping other family members with down payments on homes, education costs, marriage expenses, and other life costs, big and small.

When you pass away, whatever remains can be left to those same people as outright estate gifts or through trusts. All or part of your estate could go to nonprofits if you want. The receivers of your estate are called your *beneficiaries*, and they are named in your wills and trusts.

Legal documents use the word *beneficiary*. The rest of us think in terms of people and names. Beneficiaries could be family members, like your mother, father, cousins, children, etc. They could also be institutions, like where you went to college, your place of worship, or the agency that has cared for your family.

Primary and Contingent

The worksheets for this section have spaces for primary beneficiaries and contingent beneficiaries. Other worksheets will also use the words *primary* and *contingent* or *primary* and *successor*.

What's the difference? *Primary* is the person or people who are first in line. This is your first choice. You can have one or many primary beneficiaries. I have three children, and my estate plan splits my assets three ways—one-third for each child, with the share for my daughter with Down syndrome going to a special-needs trust. Each is a primary beneficiary. Ideally, they'll all outlive me. If that doesn't happen, my estate plan redirects the share for each child elsewhere. Where that goes depends on their ages, marital status, and whether or not they have children.

The next level is the *contingent* beneficiary. The contingent gets my assets in case the primary is not able to. That money can go to the other primary beneficiaries or anywhere else, and your attorney will map that out.

Some of the other roles are divided into primary and successor. The concept is the same. If the person I choose is incapable of performing his role, then the successor steps in. You choose the people you currently think are best, and you have a backup plan in place.

Beneficiaries

Beneficiaries are the people or organizations that will inherit your assets. They stand to "benefit" from your estate.

The primary beneficiary is the first person or group that will receive an inheritance from you. For most people, choosing primary and contingent beneficiaries is pretty simple.

A married individual usually chooses his or her spouse as the primary beneficiary.

Married people with children usually choose their children (or their trusts) as the contingent beneficiaries.

Your decision doesn't have to be more complicated than that. A good attorney will incorporate your wishes and implement the strategies needed to make this happen. The attorney might ask for one more set of contingent beneficiaries in case of disaster.

These days, there are many variations to the family model. People adopt or have children without getting married. Others get married and divorced and either stay single or get married another time. Single parents make different decisions than married ones. Some parents have children with different people. Grandparents sometimes adopt or care for grandchildren.

Naming primary and contingent beneficiaries gets more complicated with different family structures, but most people know who they want their money to go to: kids, significant others, other family members. Charities, schools, or religious groups are common beneficiaries if there is not an obvious family choice for a contingent beneficiary or to share as a primary one.

The naming of beneficiaries tends to go pretty quickly. Take a second and ask yourself, "Who do I want to get what if I pass away tomorrow?" Yes, tomorrow. Asking it that way focuses your attention. In planning, you must assume the worst.

Beneficiary Worksheet

Did certain names pop to mind? Start there. Write down the list of people on the worksheet titled "Chapter 4: Beneficiaries Worksheet."

☑ Worksheet: **Chapter 4: Beneficiaries Worksheet**

If there's one person who gets everything you own, write that name down as the primary beneficiary. If you're not sure, write down all the names of those you want to help, and review that list later. Going back to it in a day or two will help make your choice clearer, or you can talk it through with the attorney.

Don't slow yourself down if your family situation is complicated. Just get as many names on paper as needed and sort it out later. Don't stop the process from moving forward if it's unclear or doesn't feel perfect. Maybe you had children by a prior spouse and want to figure out how your current spouse and children will receive inheritances. A good attorney will help you work out the strategies and assist you with your decision-making. Keep moving for now by writing down the names of people you are considering, and it will fall into place later with advice from your professional team.

Next, write down the names of your contingent beneficiaries. These are the people and organizations that will get the inheritance if your primary beneficiaries are no longer alive.

You are reading this because you have a family member with special needs. You likely have that person as a primary or contingent beneficiary. Next to his or her name, write the word *trust* in parentheses. The share for this person will be directed to the special-needs trust. Also, if you know it, write the age of each person next to his or her name. Your attorney might recommend certain types of trusts for people under eighteen (and maybe even trusts until that person turns an age where you think she can handle money). Don't think too much about this; just get the names on paper.

The beneficiary does not do anything in your estate plan. He or she doesn't have a job to do, such as make a medical decision or distribute money. The beneficiary gets the money or property from your estate. Beneficiaries do not have to know they are named, and you can change them as needed.

Sharing Formula

In your estate plan, you get to decide who gets what and in what percentages. You can also exclude people as you see fit, and sometimes it makes sense to be specific about that. Many states require a portion of your estate to go to a spouse. Otherwise, it's all up to you.

Without a will and estate plan, you lose the right to choose who gets what. You set up a situation where expected beneficiaries might fight over the estate. Family and friends who think you promised them something appear, and it's easy for anyone and everyone to make a claim saying you made promises to them. With a will, it's clear. It's written down, notarized, and expresses your direct intentions. Without a will, a judge in your state gets to make these decisions.

As every family will be a bit different, there's no right way to split this up. The choices you make can depend on what types of assets you own. Many people own a home and have both traditional and Roth retirement accounts, life insurance, bank accounts, cars, and household and personal items. Some own business interests, land in other states, and mineral rights.

This is important work; if you have complex assets, schedule a meeting with your attorney, CPA, investment adviser, and financial planner to help sort through which assets to direct to whom. The best planning comes when you have everyone in the room at the same time.

Most people I work with keep it simple. The spouse gets it all as the primary beneficiary. The children wind up as contingents in equal percentages, with the trust in place for the family member with special needs. Some people include a charitable share and designate some percent of the estate to charities, schools, or religious institutions.

Perfect Is the Enemy of Good

It's better to have a well-drafted estate plan with slight imperfections than to have nothing. As mentioned, you can review and update your beneficiaries and make changes in your estate documents as needed. Don't forget that as you name or change beneficiaries, you must make those changes on retirement accounts, insurance products, and other assets where you've named a beneficiary by contract (ask your attorney about this).

I mentioned that beneficiaries can be organizations as well as people. Families like ours are often served by nonprofits in our community that provide services and supports like advocacy in schools, job supports, housing, food, and transportation. Many of my clients donate annually to these nonprofits; you can also leave estate gifts to provide financial support as they fulfill their missions.

Get out that worksheet and take one more look at it. Write down the names of the people (and organizations) that you want to receive some or all of your estate. The strategies will become clear to the attorney if you can articulate the who and why.

CHAPTER 5

TRUSTEES

At workshops and seminars, I often hear from people who believe they don't have enough assets to fund a trust. These people think of "trust-fund baby" when they hear the term *trust* and think it takes tens of millions of dollars to fund one. They think of trusts as something only the wealthiest of the wealthy put in place.

In special-needs planning, a trust ensures that resources stay out of your family member's name. As mentioned, adults with a qualifying disability cannot have more than $2,000 in their names; otherwise they lose SSI. Trusts are used in special-needs planning if you want to leave your family member anything more than $2,000.

Before you choose a trustee, it helps to have a basic understanding of what a trust is. A trust is simply a different way to own something (property). Some trusts allow you to control and use that property. Other types of trusts say you give up your rights to use, spend, or control that property.

You might hear the words *living*, *family*, or *revocable* before the word *trust*. These trusts hold your assets while you're alive. You can transfer money, houses, cars, and other property to these types of trusts, and nothing much changes in your financial life and in your ability to use those assets.

Right now, your bank account has your name on it. You don't even think about it. You own it, control it, and can take money out of it or put money into it. A trust is a different way to own that bank account. Instead of a bank account with a name on it (such as "John Smith's account"), the trust has its own name (such as "The Trust to Benefit John Smith" or "The John Smith Family Trust"). You get to choose the name.

Other types of trusts have different names on them and often use the word *irrevocable*. This means the funding is permanent and often for the benefit of someone other than you. In special-needs trusts, the name of the beneficiary is used in the title: "The Irrevocable Special-Needs Trust for the Benefit of Jamie Klein" or "The Sandy Allen Special-Needs Trust." It's pretty clear who the money in the trust can be used to support.

A Few Estate-Plan Basics

Estate plans commonly include a will, medical and durable powers of attorney, and trusts. Many incorporate a "living will"—a directive on whether you want to be kept on life support and under what conditions. There may be other directives, but these are the most common in special-needs planning.

A will spells out who gets your property when you die. It is your set of instructions to let everyone know who gets your "stuff"—your money, cars, jewelry, land, and other property. Simple estate plans do not include trust planning; the will gives your stuff to others. Those people get your assets outright and in their names. They choose what to do next—sell the assets, spend them, or give them to someone else.

Adding a trust changes the way someone else gets his or her share of your assets. Money does not go to your son; it goes into the trust for your son. The trust can be written to make it easy for your son to get the money, or it can be written with rules restricting access. Special-needs trusts follow governmental rules. In other types of trusts, you make the rules. For example, there might be an age rule, i.e., your son gets money at age twenty, thirty, or fifty. Or there could be lifestyle rules that say the money first goes to pay for college or cannot be paid out if your daughter has a substance-abuse issue and is not getting help.

A trust is its own entity, separate and distinct from the person who benefits from it. The trust is like a pitcher that gets filled when you put assets into it. Think of your assets as water. Water fills the pitcher (the trust). From there, someone (the trustee) pours the water into glasses. As a pitcher holds water until it's time to fill glasses, a trust holds assets until it's time to distribute them. The rules of access and distribution are written in the trust.

For our purposes, the share of your assets for your family member with special needs goes to a special-needs trust. Your family member cannot just withdraw the money; it's not like a bank account she has full access to. Someone has to manage the assets in the trust and decide when and how money can come out of the trust.

The Trustee's Job

The person in charge is the *trustee*. You get to name the trustee in your will or when you put a trust in place. The role of a trustee is a big job, you'll want to appoint someone who can handle it.

The trustee is the boss, the person in charge of the assets in the trust. In a special-needs trust, this person has full authority to buy, sell, and manage trust holdings; make distributions; file the trust's tax return; and balance current and future needs. Simple, right?

As you think about people who can handle this job, remember that the trustee does not have to, and usually does not, do all of that without help. Trustees hire professionals as needed to carry out their responsibilities for the trust.

Let's take a quick look at each of those responsibilities.

Buy, sell, and manage trust holdings. The trustee can buy or sell assets for the trust and is charged with managing them. Remember, trusts can hold just about any kind of asset. These can be simple assets, like a bank account, or complex assets, like membership interests in operating LLCs. The trust can own stocks, bonds, mutual funds, real estate, gold bars, and just about anything else. The trustee you name must be able to handle the assets in the trust. If you fund the trust with family-business shares, the trustee has to be able to read through financial statements and make entrepreneurial decisions. If the trust is mostly investment assets, you'll want someone who's familiar with how to handle them. In every case, the trustee can hire outside experts to manage portfolios, value businesses, and run those businesses. The trustee doesn't have to do it all, but the trustee has to have good enough judgment to know when help is needed and how to hire competent help.

Make distributions. The purpose of the trust is to help improve the quality of life for your family member with special needs. Benefits pay for food, shelter, and medical expenses and often provide barely enough for the basics. The trust can provide the resources necessary for your family member to have a life worth living. It can be used to buy things like tickets for Broadway shows, cell phones, furniture, vacations, clothing, and medical equipment. The trustee has to stay within the guidelines of the benefit programs that do not allow the trust to pay rent, buy groceries, or give the beneficiary cash. Your trustee must be able to learn and understand these rules so he or she can make qualified distributions.

File tax returns. Irrevocable trusts file tax returns each year. Do you have a brother who hasn't filed his return in six years? He's not the best choice for trustee. Is there a family member who files well before the April 15 deadline and who has organized folders with all the supporting documents? That would be a better choice. The trustee does not have to prepare taxes and can hire a professional to do it.

Plan for the future. It's easy to spend money quickly. I've had several clients who've received an inheritance or settlement and burned through it in less than a year. I've also had many who handle their money better. The best advice I heard about how to handle an inheritance came from a father to his son when the son got money from a trust at age thirty. The father said, "Use the money to buy things that can increase in value." The son worked and didn't need the money in the short term.

Trustees supporting people living on benefits have to decide how much to spend in the short term to improve life and how to have money available in the future. Those are tough decisions. The trustee can hire a financial planner to map out a strategy that includes a spending and investment plan.

Characteristics of a Good Trustee

The next exercise has you write down the names of people you'd appoint as trustee for your family. As names come to mind, remember that you want someone who can handle the technical details listed above and who has the character traits to do it.

The trustee is bound to act in the sole interest of the beneficiary. The money in the trust is for your family member with a disability and not anyone else. The trustee can be paid for time spent and can hire experts to assist, but the funds are not to be spent improving the trustee's life.

Your trustee cannot have divided loyalties. He or she acts only for the betterment of the beneficiary.

Because your trustee will perform tasks for your family member with a disability, you want that person to have the spirit of service.

Your trustee cannot be an expert in everything required; he or she has to have enough knowledge to understand the scope of tasks and the ability to make good hires for the experts. Love, hope, and compassion do not constitute competence, although it would be fantastic to find someone who is both competent and caring.

Personal or Corporate Trustee

Many years ago, a couple came into my office to talk about special-needs planning. We discussed the purpose of the special-needs trust and the role of the trustee. I asked my usual question: "Do you have anybody in your family who can be the trustee?" The husband and wife looked at each other with expressions of sadness and then looked back at me. They told me they had three children—one with a disability, one in jail, and another who spent every penny she got and then some. They did not have anyone in their family with the attributes needed to handle the job. The siblings did not have any integrity, a desire to serve others, or anything close to competence with finances.

They did not have a family member who could serve in the role of trustee and were at a loss as to what to do next.

In past generations, the common practice was to appoint a bank as trustee, and many community banks thrived in the trust business. This practice has shifted toward personal trustees—a family member or friend who can mix their love for the beneficiary with the work to be done. Both options are available; today, you can appoint either a personal or corporate trustee.

A *personal trustee* is a friend or family trustee who knows you and your children and can make decisions based on the needs and wants of your family. Because of the close bond, there's a different feeling with a personal trustee—a sense of confidence that the trustee will work hard for your family member.

The *corporate trustee* brings a different skill set to the work. These institutions specialize in trust work, understand how to get the technical work done, and take the time to learn the rules governing special-needs trusts. You shouldn't be concerned with their competence. Banks are not the only option for a corporate trustee—there are now independent trustees and trust companies that can work with your existing financial and legal team.

Even though the trend is toward naming personal trustees, there's no right choice. The circumstances differ with every family based on the ages of siblings, how people in your world manage their own lives, and the desire to have caring, known people versus those who might better handle complex assets.

Trustee Worksheet

Take out the next worksheet, "Chapter 5: Trustee Worksheet." Write down the names of those who might be the best persons or organizations to act on behalf of your family member.

☑ Worksheet: **Chapter 5: Trustee Worksheet**

Does anyone stand out? Maybe there are a few. Write their names down. Put them in order of who you think is best, second best, and so on. You can talk through this decision with your attorney. If no one fits, then ask your financial and legal professionals for names of corporate trustees.

CHAPTER 6

GUARDIANS

New parents don't often think about the legal and ethical duties that come with having a baby. They make funny faces, feed babies all kinds of mushed vegetables, and change diapers. Parents are overly tired from lack of sleep and walk around in a daze, barely able to function. Who has the brainpower to think about what requirements need to be in place in eighteen years if that newborn cannot make medical decisions on her own?

The focus at the time of birth is on health and safety; teaching basics like walking, talking, and the ABCs; and singing songs. Parents don't report to anyone (well, maybe their in-laws), and they don't think too much about the legal responsibility that comes with having a newborn.

Then comes the age of eighteen.

For families with special-needs members, eighteen is a major milestone. It's the time our legal rights end and we have to focus on the best way to support family members who likely have a reduced ability to make important decisions. Age eighteen is the time to ask whether your child can choose where to live, understand medical issues and treatment options, handle money, and eat healthfully. Most parents of children with special needs know their children will need help navigating our complex world.

The list of ways I need to help my daughter is long. My daughter cannot yet drive and needs help with transportation to school programs, doctor appointments, and activities. She cannot reach the pedals at age seventeen, and she's stopped growing; it's unlikely she will get her license anytime soon. She will need support with transportation for her lifetime.

She doesn't know the difference in value between a dollar bill and a twenty-dollar bill. She's had plenty of education about money in school, and I've taken her to stores for practical experience. The numbers just don't add up for her. Sometimes this brings great happiness. She sets up lemonade stands when the weather is good and does a brisk business. Her excitement is always high whether the customer gives her fifty cents or ten dollars for the cookie or glass of lemonade. We love those big tippers! She loves the interaction as much as the actual value of the money she makes, but I don't see her balancing her budget.

My daughter needs help getting to the doctor's office and understanding the purpose of the visit and the update from the doctor. She has a blood draw quarterly to check her thyroid function, and if it were up to her, she would just skip these visits. None of us really wants a blood draw, but we do it because of the health outcomes we desire. My daughter does not make the connection between the blood draw and her health as well as she could, so she needs help in every way to ensure she has the right medicine in the right dose.

Adults with intellectual and developmental disabilities need assistance in ways our other family members do not. Someone will have to be responsible for making sure our family members are well cared for. This is the role of a guardian.

Guardian

The role of *guardian* is something parents take on without thinking about it when they have a child. There's a social, legal, and ethical responsibility to that child. It's called *parenting*.

That changes when a child turns eighteen. Somehow, that tiny little baby you know and love is a fully functioning, legal entity recognized by state and federal governments. It's a shock. That child still lives at home, barely cleans her room, and is dependent on you for three healthy meals a day, a place to live, and someone to pay for gas—but technically, that person is a legal adult.

It's true for every child, including those with disabilities.

It's hard to imagine any eighteen-year-old making informed decisions when presented with complex choices; that's especially true for people who have intellectual and developmental disabilities.

As mentioned, a person who turned eighteen is a legal adult. She can open a bank account, join the military, and make medical decisions. She can decide where to live, what to eat, and how to dress. (This last one happens much earlier—just try telling your sixteen-year-old what to wear to school!) These young people don't make the best decisions all the time, but at eighteen, they get to make them.

Our country has developed a system to help people who cannot make decisions on their own. In these cases, the courts appoint a person to act on behalf of another. We use the word *guardian*.

A court-appointed guardian has the legal authority and duty to care for another person. In many ways, the guardian acts like a parent; the guardian takes responsibility for someone else's health and well-being. The guardian does not have to do everything; he or she can choose to oversee the process and work performed by others.

A *guardian* and *conservator* are both positions that must be appointed by a judge (or another legal authority). Each state uses these terms differently. For clarity, I use the terms to mean different roles for different purposes. In my work, *guardian* refers to the person appointed by a court to take care of someone else's health and well-being. *Conservator* refers to a court-appointed person who helps with money. A conservator is basically a court-appointed trustee. Good planning on your part preempts the need for a conservator, and since the goal of this book is good planning, I'm not going to review that role.

Parents can first request to become the guardian for their family member with a disability when that person turns age eighteen. The process requires an application to the court, which then reviews your ability to act as a guardian. If you've been a positive influence in your child's life and have taken care of your responsibilities toward your child, it's pretty straightforward.

Advocates for adults with special needs have changed the way we think about guardianship for the better. Appointing someone as guardian means taking rights from that person; if I am guardian for my daughter in *all* capacities, then she cannot act on her own to get medical care and manage other areas of her life. She is not able to decide what type of medical treatments to have or where to live, for example.

Instead of complete guardianship, some families work with their children as coguardians and use this blended style to make decisions together.

Take out the chapter 6 "Guardian Worksheet." It has a place for the primary guardian. Most likely, this is you, your spouse, or your partner. Put that name in the first spot.

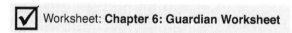

Worksheet: **Chapter 6: Guardian Worksheet**

Successor Guardian

The next worksheet guides you to identify a *successor guardian*, which is someone who can step in as guardian when you either pass away or can no longer act in that role. This is the person (or people) you think could best take over for you.

Unlike a successor trustee, you cannot just name a successor guardian and have that person go to work. Courts appoint guardians, and the new person has to apply, just like you did. Still, it helps to identify the people you want to be involved because the court will take that into consideration. While you are still alive, you can petition the court for the successor to step in, and you can be a witness to the qualities and experiences of your desired successor.

Avoid surprises. Don't name a person without first talking to him or her. Your sister in another state who does not have children might be a great person, but she might not be willing to take the responsibility that comes with the job. Maybe your brother is taking a new job in a different country, and now is not the time for him to step in if needed. Those are just a couple of examples of some of the practical reasons to consider.

Do you want your guardian to be someone who is not ready or willing or who doesn't feel able to handle the job? Of course not. You want someone committed to the task, not someone who will feel burdened by it. It's never a good thing for a guardian to start off feeling resentment, surprise, fear, or anxiety. It's better to find someone who expresses a willingness to step in.

For aging parents who are guardians, there are two other steps to consider.

First, you can work with the court to appoint a coguardian. This person shares the job with you today and gives you the chance to educate the new person on what it is you do. The coguardian will have the chance to get to know the day-to-day life of your family member, review medical documents, and take some of the workload before having it all to do on his or her own. This gives everyone a chance to make sure it works. After all, the person with a disability comes first, and you want to know that the guardian will do everything possible to make life fantastic for him or her.

Another option is to raise the issue of the successor guardian in the annual report to the court. In my state, the form has a section asking if the guardianship needs to continue, if there are any recommended changes, and if you wish to remain as guardian. Another section asks for recommended changes. This is a great place to identify the need for a successor or coguardian and to name that person.

As guardian, you are the court-appointed person making certain decisions for someone else. In the eyes of the court, you are the key person, and your voice matters when it comes to decisions for the future. Identifying a coguardian or future guardian and providing some explanation as to why that person is your best choice will help with future transitions.

Write on the chapter 6 "Guardian Worksheet" the names of the people you'd most like to act as successor guardian.

Three More Jobs. One More Document.

Estate-planning documents will ask you to name individuals or entities to fill three more roles: a *personal representative*, a *medical power of attorney*, and a *general power of attorney*. Your attorney will also talk to you about a *living will*.

Personal Representative

Terms in estate planning make me laugh. Is there any day of the week you'd willingly walk into a room with an executor? It makes me think of a spy movie in which the "executor" is ready to fire a pistol with a silencer or of a western movie with a hanging judge. Whatever it is, I want to avoid the executor.

Somewhere along the way, the title *executor* changed to *personal representative*. That's a much kinder and gentler title and one more descriptive of the role. Unlike an executor, I could use a personal representative pretty much every day—I'd send my personal representative to the Department of Motor Vehicles, to the supermarket, or to get gas. I'd turn over everything I don't want to do to my personal representative.

In estate planning, the personal representative steps in when you pass away and is the person or institution authorized to finalize your estate.

There's a lot of work to be done after you die. There's money to distribute to the beneficiaries. Filings must be made with appropriate state entities. Creditors demand information from the estate. A final tax return gets filed. Bills get paid so your house, cars, and other property remain in your name until distributed to beneficiaries.

All of these tasks fall to the personal representative. As with selecting a trustee, you'll want someone who can handle the job—someone who is organized and can manage a checkbook, taxes and government reporting. Right now, while you are alive, you pay your insurances, mortgage, utilities, and other bills. There will be a period of time when these bills will still need to get paid after your death. Another big part of the job is tax and legal reporting. Think about the people in your life who you think can take over for you, and write down their names.

Remember that the personal representative does more than just pay your final bills; it's possible that some serious people skills will be needed.

Choices you made in your estate plan could cause hurt feelings, anger, or disappointment among family and friends. Even though you choose who gets what, others may be expecting something different.

Anyone can contest or challenge your estate. Maybe one child expected to get more money or the family home even though you decided to leave those assets to the special-needs trust. If your documents are solid, recent, and have been drafted with an attorney who had you sign everything in front of witnesses, then it's unlikely that person can sue and win. But the person can still sue. A personal representative with good people skills can help each beneficiary understand how and when you finalized your estate documents and help them navigate the emotional roller coaster that comes with grieving a family member and understanding an inheritance. Good people skills are not a requirement, but they don't hurt.

Again, as with the other roles we've talked about, once you've decided on who you think will best fill the role of personal representative, talk to that person to see if she wants the job. Most people will feel a bit insecure about taking on the role, but you can reassure them they can hire competent help. If your first choice simply refuses, then find someone else. Name your primary and successors as you did with your trustee and guardian.

It's likely you will choose the same person for trustee and personal representative—the type of skill set needed is similar for each role. Use the chapter 7 "Personal Representative Worksheet" for these names.

☑ Worksheet: **Chapter 6: Personal Representative**

Powers of Attorney

The American Automobile Association released a study in 2018 revealing that 75 percent of all motorists considered themselves above-average drivers—a statistical impossibility. Even if you are in that better half of drivers, you still have the other drivers to worry about. If you get in an accident and are unconscious, you'll need someone to authorize medical care and to work with the doctors. For this, you will need a medical power of attorney—someone who can act on your behalf. If you remain in the hospital and need your bills paid, your investments reviewed, and your house sold, another type of POA is needed: a general power of attorney.

When you die, the personal representative steps in to handle your estate. That job starts after you are deceased. You might need someone to act on your behalf while you're still alive but cannot, for whatever reason, act or make decisions. That person is given power—called a *power of attorney* (POA)—to act for you in specific circumstances.

Most estate documents include both a general POA and a medical POA.

General POA

As mentioned, the general POA handles financial and legal decisions on your behalf. You can give that person full rights, or you can limit their rights to specific circumstances. You will need this person to step in if you're incapacitated, and you can write into the documents when the powers of attorney can be used. These powers end when you die.

Let's say you put an offer on a house, have been waiting to close, and it's taking longer than expected. Months earlier, you booked a family trip to Maine, and now the closing and the vacation are scheduled for the same time. What do you do? You can give another person a *limited* POA to close the real estate deal. This person can use the POA to sign the real estate closing documents. This limited POA does not give that person access to your bank or investment accounts, but it does give him or her the right to act for you in a limited way so you get to buy your new home.

With a general POA, you give someone else far more authority to act. A broadly written general POA will let someone else handle *every* financial or legal transaction on your behalf. That person can go to the bank and take out your money, pay your bills online, or sign documents to sell your house. The POA has an obligation to act in your best interests and on your behalf, like a trustee.

Obviously, you want to find a trustworthy person who will act in your best interests and who is good at making decisions.

Many times, estate documents are written so that a general POA starts when something specific, such as an accident, happens, and you are incapacitated and need help; in these cases, it provides a safeguard. It's not to be used at all times; it springs into action in certain circumstances. As mentioned, the power of attorney ends when you die.

Medical POA

Medical POAs are equally important. You can choose the same person for both medical and financial needs, or you can choose a different person for each task, depending on their different skill sets and temperaments. Remember the choice between a guardian and trustee? I tend to think of a guardian as someone with the compassion and love of a second-grade teacher—someone willing to see the world through the eyes of your family member with a disability. The trustee has that banker ability with numbers and taxes.

There's a similar distinction between the medical POA and financial POA. Some people just understand how to make medical decisions. Technical medical language doesn't overwhelm them, and the fast pace of a hospital or emergency room isn't an issue for them. They manage to keep the most important issues clear and are able to balance the impact of taking action or waiting to gather more information before making a decision.

Financial matters move at a different pace—a bill can be paid on Tuesday, Wednesday, or Thursday and the time lag won't have an impact. A decision to authorize surgery or a medical intervention often cannot be put off without consequences. The financial POA's organizational skills are paramount as bills and payments happen over time; the medical POA, on the other hand, may have to make tough, quick, emotional decisions regarding health.

Medical POAs spring into action when a person cannot make medical decisions for himself or herself. Heart attacks, car accidents, and other sudden injuries are circumstances where the medical POA might be needed.

Living Will

There is one more document you'll need to be familiar with before heading to your attorney's office: the *living will*. This document spells out your wishes for receiving medical care in a situation where it's unclear whether you will recover or not.

In a living will, you indicate whether or not you want to remain on life support under certain conditions. This set of circumstances differs from the duties of the medical POA. That person authorizes treatment and care, often acting in emergency situations. Once the emergency ends, it's possible that recovery does not continue and you remain in a coma and that your life depends on the assistance of breathing, feeding, and circulatory technologies. The living will provides direction on whether you wish to remain this way, with the slim hope of recovery, or reduce technological support with the likelihood of your demise.

Unlike the other chapters and exercises in this book, you don't name anyone in your living will, and yet the document is 100 percent about the people in your life.

This is not a decision anyone wants to make on your behalf. The living will gives those you love your direction and support and removes the guilt and anxiety that accompany the decision of whether to continue life support or not. By putting forth your wishes, you take some of the burden off the people around you.

Worksheet

Take out the chapter 7 "General POA" and "Medical POA" worksheets and write down your preferred choices. Again, you don't have to worry about the order of your preferences on the first draft, but you can always pencil in a 1, 2, or 3 to indicate those preferences. These are not final decisions; they are guidelines to help you get started as you work with your attorney. Name successors for each of these roles.

☑ Worksheet: **Chapter 6: General POA**

☑ Worksheet: **Chapter 6: Medical POA**

CHAPTER 7

CHOOSING AN ATTORNEY

Congratulations! Having completed the worksheets, you've made significant progress and taken the time to understand the critical people who will be incorporated into your estate plan with a special-needs trust. Bring those worksheets with you as you take the next step—meeting with an attorney.

An estate-planning attorney is someone who works with wills, trusts, and probate and who is familiar with the unique planning that happens when SSI, Medicaid, and other governmental benefits need to be secured and maintained.

There are many attorneys in every community. Some handle land issues; others water rights. Head to the local courthouse and you will find district attorneys and those specializing in criminal defense, DUIs, and personal injury. These types of attorneys can't help you put together your estate plan. You need a specialist.

Your brother-in-law or friend from college might be a great attorney in his or her chosen field, but don't hire one of them to set up your trust unless they're also an expert in special-needs trusts. While all this may seem obvious, many people want to get the work done quickly and cheaply and consequently turn to the wrong advisers for help.

To begin your search for an attorney, ask people you trust who they've used. Cast a wide net. Ask friends and other parents of children with special needs as you see them at local events, at therapy appointments, and at school. Don't stop there. Ask your CPA and financial adviser for the names of people they like and recommend. Ask the service organizations and nonprofits you work with who they know and like as well. It's likely you will hear names repeated. That doesn't mean a person whose name you hear repeatedly is the best or the best for you, but it's a great place to start.

There's no reason to conduct a big search if you already have a good attorney. When my son was born, we had a local attorney draft our estate plan. When my daughter was born with Down syndrome, I went back to this attorney and asked her about her knowledge and experience with special-needs trusts. It turns out she knew them quite well, and she updated our documents to reflect the change in my family. Easy and done.

Most estate-planning attorneys will meet with you at no charge or for a reduced consultation fee for the first meeting. They want to get to know you as much as you want to interview them.

The "Chapter 8: Choosing an Attorney Worksheet" has a list of questions to ask as you interview prospective attorneys. Feel free to add more questions as they come up. Take these questions with you to the meeting. I've had plenty of people come to my office with a list of questions to ask a financial planner. It's great to know that people are doing their homework, and they wind up being better clients because they find someone who meets their needs. Ask each attorney you talk with the same questions so you can understand what that attorney can do for you, how that person charges, and whether you think the attorney can help your family.

The attorney does not have to be your new best friend; the attorney will perform work for you, and it's unlikely you will be back for another five years. That being said, it's a bonus when you like the attorney and feel like that person can do good work and make it enjoyable for you and your family.

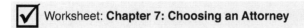 Worksheet: **Chapter 7: Choosing an Attorney**

People have told me they feel intimidated before coming to my office. They just don't know what to expect, and often their image of a financial planner is someone who loves numbers and not people. A good planner needs to love both. I've heard people express even more anxiety about meeting with an attorney. The bad attorney jokes and tough attorneys on TV turn people off. Most estate-planning attorneys want to help and are sincere about serving their clients' needs and not their own egos and image. You will quickly know after meeting with a few attorneys which one is right for you.

You'll definitely want someone who listens to your needs and concerns. Every situation is different, and every trust or plan has unique elements.

One person who came to my office expressed concern that her son would look shabby once he started receiving benefits. In her mind, people with developmental disabilities wear out-of-date clothes with ragged edges. She did not want that for her son, and she wanted some language in her estate plan to show that trust funds could and should be used to keep his wardrobe fresh and attractive. Others have thought they wanted the family home to go to nonprofits when the trust beneficiary passed and needed help from their planning team to identify the right people and the right strategies to make this happen. Express your preferences and let the attorney incorporate them into the trust as long as those preferences do not conflict with benefit rules.

Find an attorney who understands special-needs planning and is right for you. There's no need to compromise.

Don't let this step hold you back. It's likely you have people penciled in for all the other roles in your plan. Pick up the phone, fire off an email, or type out a text right now and get in touch with three people who can give you attorney recommendations. Do the same tomorrow. By the end of the week, you will have enough names of attorneys you can call and interview.

Write the time and day you will meet with these attorneys on the "Commitment Dates Worksheet" from chapter 3.

☑ Worksheet: **Chapter 3: Commitment Dates**

CHAPTER 8

GETTING ORGANIZED

One woman I know kept a table near her front door. That table was the centerpiece of her organizational system. Important mail came in the postal slot near the front door and got piled on one end of the table as it arrived. Over time, new mail was piled on top of the old pile. As more mail arrived, she pushed the pile down the table to make room for the recent arrivals. It was a simple system, and everything was available.

This isn't the system I recommend, it's not the best one I've heard of, and yet it worked. It wasn't the most effective system for organization and access, but every significant account statement was there when needed (and it was almost never needed).

Getting prepared for an appointment with your attorney is one time when those statements are needed.

Before you meet with your attorney, get organized by collecting your legal and financial records.

Everyone has a different record-keeping system. Whether yours resembles your teenage son's room after a tornado or an Apple store the day before a product launch (with everything in its place and a place for everything) will determine whether getting your records organized will be simple or laborious. You don't have to make a permanent change to whatever works for you. You will need some intense, temporary focus to make the estate planning process go quickly with positive results.

Today, many of us have gone digital, so we don't get those piles of papers clogging our desks and tables. That does not always mean we have easy access to our accounts. For the most part, we use email addresses for usernames, but finding, remembering, and updating passwords is an endless, mundane task. Two-factor authentication makes our accounts safer; it also makes getting into some websites that much more annoying.

Whatever it takes, get your documents together. Sign in to your accounts, dig through old mail, and unpack the one box that contains everything from your last move.

Tax and Distribution Planning

To your professional team, financial documents are like puzzle pieces. Before any work can be done, the pieces must be laid out in full view. Puzzlers start with the edges because they provide structure and guidance and anchor the rest of the work.

Current documents give attorneys and financial planners crucial information that can help guide them in assisting you. It's important to make estimates about the overall size of your estate; the starting point for that is your current net worth, which is calculated by adding up all your assets and subtracting your debts. Some assets are better than others for funding trusts due to the tax code or the ability to sell or manage the assets. Traditional retirement accounts owe taxes on distribution that impact the end value received by an heir or trust. Real estate takes time to sell, and your plan may need to balance the need for people to receive cash quickly or over time. Business interests create additional challenges that will impact your choice of trustee. Don't spend time analyzing how each asset will be used in your estate plan; just assemble something that shows what you have.

Let the team of your attorney, CPA, and financial planner guide you through how to direct your assets. Don't get caught up now in all the choices you can make. Remember, speed is important here, and there's no reason to have every question answered before you even know if the questions are important and necessary to your planning.

Review of Current Beneficiary Designations

Some accounts have beneficiary designations that you signed when you opened those accounts. Retirement accounts and life-insurance products today almost always require you to name beneficiaries when you open them. These assets pass outside your will and trust planning.

After you finalize your estate plan, go back to the accounts with beneficiary designations and review and update them so they align with your new plan. I've met with people who have 401(k) accounts with multiple prior employers. Each time they took a new job, they signed up for a new plan. The old accounts stayed with the previous employers' plans, leaving money in many different places. In some cases, these people have had to call the human resources departments to find out if there was money in the old plan and were happily surprised to find there were funds. For families with special-needs members, this could be disastrous, as those forgotten accounts could lead to an inheritance worth more than $2,000 going to a person with a qualifying disability.

Life changes. New graduates working their first post-college jobs who don't have significant others or spouses often choose their parents and siblings as beneficiaries on their first retirement accounts. In a few years, those new workers might get married and have children, but the beneficiary designation does not follow those life changes. This can also be true when people get divorced or when a beneficiary dies—there's not an automatic change made to the beneficiary designations on life-insurance or retirement accounts.

At this step, having the account statements and financial data is enough to get started. Don't spend too much time tracking down the beneficiary documentation. Most likely, you will go back and update this after your estate plan is done.

Online access makes it easier to locate current beneficiary designations. If you have to log in to get a recent account statement for your 401(k), click two or three more times to see who you have listed as the beneficiary and record that on the statement.

All Assets and Liabilities

Every asset and liability factors into your financial and estate plan.

Debts must be paid after you pass away, so compile a list of yours. Again, depending on whether your record-keeping looks like a tornado hit your living room or it's been organized by Jeeves the butler, you can prepare for your meeting in different ways. You can list your debts on a scrap of paper. Write "mortgage," and next to it write the dollar amount remaining on that loan. Do the same with each credit card, student loan, or other debt. Your estate planner will want the remaining balance (how much you owe). Your financial planner will be interested in the interest rate for each loan, when it started, whether the loan has a designated payoff time (like a mortgage), and your monthly payment. If you are super organized, bring all the statements to your meeting with the attorney.

The same can be true for your assets. You don't need your closing statement from when you bought the house; just write down an estimate of its current value. You can get a good estimate by going to an online real-estate site. This won't be exact, but it will be good enough to use as you start your planning. Write down what you paid for each asset next to its current value. Do the same for any cars, other real estate, business interests, or household goods. The exact value is not needed for this first meeting or to get things started. If you don't have specific information, that's okay; just list the assets you own.

Checklist

Use the chapter 8 "Getting Organized Checklist" to jog your memory. Some financial tools, like stock options and term life insurance, do not have present value and are used to generate assets in the future if certain conditions are met. Make sure to include these.

One benefit of taking the time for this temporary organization is that you might find assets you forgot about, including accounts from past jobs where you made retirement-plan contributions. This regularly happens to people and it always surprises me when it does. I know each of my accounts and always have a basic idea of what's in each and what it's worth. But, then, I am a financial planner who loves spreadsheets.

Get all the applicable statements, and once your estate plan is in place, take steps to consolidate those assets into fewer accounts under your control.

PART 2

NEXT STEPS

CHAPTER 9

COMMUNICATE YOUR PLAN

American artist Samuel F. B. Morse invented an early version of his famous code around 1837. Almost fifty years later, Alexander Graham Bell received the first patent for what we now call the telephone. Ray Tomlinson is credited as the inventor of email in 1971. Today, we instant message through social media apps; call people, email them, video chat with our phones; text and call on our watches; and conduct group meetings through any number of platforms. We do not lack for ways to communicate.

An important part of your planning involves letting others know what you've done, even if you're not asking for their assistance or approval.

My planning methods focus on actions *you* can take. Setting up a trust, eliminating debt, and saving for the future, for example, do not require anyone else's input or approval. The estate plan doesn't need to be sanctioned by a committee, it doesn't require a consensus among extended family, and it doesn't have to take long to put in place. You make the commitment. You gather the financial and legal statements. You call the attorney and sign the documents. You can get it done quickly.

Estate planning does not end when you sign your documents and walk out of the attorney's office. Kind, considerate, and helpful people can spoil your planning if you do not inform them of your work. Your next step starts when you pick up the phone or write an email to the people in your family and social circle explaining the work you've done, its value, and the importance of SSI and Medicaid in creating a high-quality life for your family member with special needs.

Introvert or Extrovert?

This won't be a problem for those who've told everyone in the universe about their estate plans. Does this sound like you? Are you someone who processes new information by talking with everyone and anyone? People like you have already told their parents, siblings, friends, the neighbor's dog, and anyone within speaking distance that they have a family member with special needs and are now taking steps to protect that family member's benefits. One advantage these people have is they gather incredible amounts of information that can be used to shape and inform their planning. They've also already communicated what they are doing, and so no one will be surprised when they come back and ask for assistance in making sure those plans are effective. I will come back to this.

Or does this sound like you? You keep your head down. You read, research, gather the information, do the work, and then move on. People like you do not need much input from others and feel that even whispering their intentions to friends and neighbors or saying the words, "special-needs trust" out loud will slow down the process. This intensity can be a great strategy to get stuff done as it's unlikely there will be a delay in taking action once the timeline is determined and work has commenced. The downside is that when it is time to let others know about the work, about its importance, and about what assistance might be needed, it will come as a surprise to everyone they talk to.

Whatever your style—processing aloud or quiet focus—you will want to have a structured, meaningful conversation with the people most likely to want to give a gift or leave an inheritance to your son or daughter with a qualifying disability.

Potential Pitfalls

Consider the following scenarios:

It's graduation time. Your daughter with special needs is a high school senior. She's picked up her cap and gown at the school, and you are preparing to host a party with family and friends to celebrate her achievement. She turned eighteen a few months earlier, and the first deposit of her SSI income sits in the bank account you've established to receive those funds. You have access to this representative payee account and can spend the money to support your daughter, but it is her money. You've helped her buy new shoes with that money, and $700 remains.

After the party, you open greeting cards from the twenty relatives who came, and each card holds a check made out to your daughter. Your parents gifted $750. Same with your in-laws. That's $1,500. Your husband's family and your brothers and sisters each gave her $100, which equals another $500. The money from friends combined equals another $500. It's quite the haul, and you stop for a moment of appreciation as you cannot quite believe how generous they have all been.

Then you do the math. The gifts add up to $2,500. Your daughter has $700 in her account. In total, she has $3,200 of countable resources in her name—$1,200 more than the $2,000 resource limit. She is in danger of losing her SSI income benefit and the automatic qualification for her state and federally supported Medicaid benefits that come with it.

If you don't take action, your daughter will lose her SSI, Medicaid and state funded benefits and she will not be able to participate in the day program you recently lined up to start next month.

There's an easy fix here, and it will be highlighted in Chapter 12: "Emergencies." This money can be spent, placed in a pooled-income trust, or deposited into an ABLE Act account. All told, in this example, the gifts total $1,200 over the resource limit and it could be spent quickly to buy a new phone or computer, or to change your daughter's wardrobe, or upgrade furniture, or pay for a trip. $1,200 is fairly easy to spend.

This next scenario showcases a bigger problem. Your older brother unexpectedly passes away. For much of his life, he traveled the world as a sports photographer even as he kept a home base in Boston, where he had a steady career teaching at a local university. He never married and did not have children. He was frugal, contributed to his retirement accounts, and for some reason had a term life-insurance policy, even though he didn't have anyone depending on his income. He's listed your thirty-year-old son with a developmental disability as the sole beneficiary of his estate and you just found out that he left your son $500,000.

At first, you are thankful and proud of your brother for his kindness and ability to save. That $500,000 will go far, and the news comes just as you are finding out that your son's health might be improved by a week of intensive medical care at a specialty clinic, which, unfortunately, Medicaid will not cover. The cost of that treatment is $25,000. It's a bittersweet moment as you mourn your brother but at the same time realize you can now help your son.

Then you remember the $2,000 resource limit. Your son lives in a host home, and his living costs are paid by a state program and SSI. His high medical needs are funded by Medicaid. The total cost of his care exceeds

$75,000 per year and is expected to be this high for decades. If he receives this money, he will lose his benefit programs until he spends the inheritance. It is likely that he will have to move home to be cared for by you as his nonprofit does not have a mechanism to receive private payments. Once the money is gone, he can reapply for benefits.

Again, there are solutions to problems like this, but it costs time and money and peace of mind for everyone involved.

Anxiety or Opportunity?

In both cases, simple communication could have prevented the money from being gifted to or left to your family member. There are important conversations to have with others as you finalize your estate plan to avoid situations where money is given to your family member.

Take time to think about how you can talk to family and close friends about your estate plan and about any hurdles you might face in having that conversation. Start by explaining that you have updated your estate plan (say updating your *will* if *estate plan* sounds too fancy) to help protect your family member with a disability. Use this person's name—a lot. Your update and planning are not about you. You are not asking for a gift or to be included in their will. You are providing information to someone else— your mom, dad, aunt, or uncle, for example—with the hope that they will understand the importance of benefits so they can adjust their plans if those plans conflict with preserving governmental benefits.

Ideally, you are talking to people who care about you, love your entire family, and are willing to help you. Once they hear about the value of benefits and the actions you've taken to preserve them, they can consider fixes to their planning.

This has happened in my life. In drafting new estate documents, my sister-in-law and her husband understood that any money they might leave to my daughter had to go to her special-needs trust, so my sister-in-law called and asked for the specific language she should use in her documents. I called my attorney for that information, forwarded it to my sister-in-law, and avoided a future crisis. This short series of calls and emails did not take much time—maybe ten to fifteen minutes, all told.

Some of you reading this may have difficult family situations or come from families who never talk about money. You may feel certain that any attempt at communication will fail. Dad will change the subject, Mom will find something else to do, your brother will think you are asking for a loan. For some, the relationship is too strained for a call.

You have two options. You do not have to reach out to family and friends. The results of poor planning can be fixed with additional time and expense that could have been avoided, but it's not required that everyone fix what they've done. If the thought of talking with family members about your situation gives you more anxiety than having to fix the problem down the road, then just don't do it.

The other option is to give it a try. Take this as an opportunity to gain a new skill or increase personal confidence as you force yourself to engage with your family in a new and different way. As parents of those with qualifying disabilities, we have had and will have plenty of opportunities to develop and improve our advocacy skills. At school, the annual IEP meeting requires that we advocate and educate school staff about what is best for our children. And many families interact with the Social Security Administration or Medicaid offices in their states for regular financial reviews. This process requires families to organize documents and explain how funds are used, and as a result, we learn how to manage our finances better.

Education, Not Expectation

Take the challenge of talking with your family as another opportunity to raise your advocacy skills. Write out the critical points you want to make; rehearse the conversation with your spouse or partner. Take a deep breath, sit down with your parents and siblings, and outline the reasons you've updated your plan, explaining the value of benefits and the importance of all this for your son or daughter.

Remember that you cannot force people to change their plans. Attempt to hold these conversations free of the expectation that your family members will make changes or that they will immediately understand the importance of your planning and how they can help. How long was it from when *you* first heard the words "special-needs trust" before you picked up the phone to set an appointment with an attorney? Don't expect anyone else to move faster than you did, even if you are now motivated to finalize every detail.

Educate your family about the importance of what you've done and, if they show interest, how they can help. Remember, it's their choice whether they do something or not. And that's okay. You have done your part in laying out the case and educating them. Let them decide what to do, and be prepared to help if they say yes today or at a time in the future.

CHAPTER 10

UPDATE BENEFICIARY DESIGNATIONS

One woman called my office seeking help. Her mother had died recently, and the estate was being settled. Her sister with qualifying disabilities was going to receive part of the inheritance, in her name. Was there anything that could be done to avoid this?

Prior to her death, Mom had worked with an attorney to include special-needs provisions in her estate plan. She intended to leave her assets in equal shares to each of her children with the share of her IRA, home, and bank accounts for the daughter with disabilities directed to the special-needs trust. Perfect, right?

Unfortunately, no.

Mom had transferred her investment and retirement accounts to a new adviser a few years prior to her passing. Though her retirement-account beneficiary form was handled as the attorney directed and the share of this account went to the special-needs trust, there was another account—a taxable investment account. To this account, Mom and the adviser had added transfer on death (TOD) provisions, and on the corresponding form, Mom had named each child, as an individual, as an heir. The share for the family member with disabilities went to her and not to the trust. For some reason, the IRA form had been handled correctly, while the new TOD form had not. Mom hadn't worked with the rest of her planning team during the transfer. There hadn't been a second set of eyes reviewing the documents. The chance to avoid the mistake was lost.

A TOD acts as a beneficiary form for investment accounts and has the same legal force as a beneficiary designation—it's a contract between the account owner and heirs that allows for the direct transfer of an estate. Mom signed the TOD and included the daughter with special needs along with others. A quick signature led to an oversight that caused stress for the family and endangered benefits.

All of a sudden, the daughter who'd been receiving benefits had money in her name and was in danger of losing those benefits, even though Mom had tried to do everything correctly.

She'd worked with an estate attorney skilled in special-needs work.

Her will had been drafted correctly and her assets had been passed to the special-needs trust for this daughter. The IRA beneficiary form had named the trust as the recipient of the share for this daughter.

Mom did not have any life insurance or other assets designated to pass by contract. She no longer owned a home, but if she had, the share of the home would have passed through the language in the will and gone to the trust.

The TOD account, regrettably, directed close to $65,000 to this adult individual receiving SSI and Medicaid-funded services, an amount *far* above the $2,000 resource limit. Although $65,000 was not insignificant, it was not nearly enough to replace the value of her monthly income, host-home living, and health insurance and community benefits for long.

This could have been avoided. Luckily, it was fixable. We'll discuss some options for fixes in Chapter 12-Emergencies.

Reviewing Your Accounts

It's important you review the title and beneficiary designation on each of the accounts you have in place. Mistakes like the one discussed above are easy enough to avoid by taking a few simple steps, as outlined below. (You can ask your attorney and financial adviser for additional help with these steps.)

Step 1

You gathered your statements in the "Getting Organized" chapter from the first part of this book, so they should be easy to find. With these statements in front of you, list each asset you own on a piece of paper or in an electronic document. Put the following column headers at the top of the page in this order: Asset, Value, Asset Owner(s), Type, Primary Beneficiary, Contingent Beneficiary.

If you cannot locate the information for one of these categories or are unsure about something, leave that part blank. Real estate, investment accounts, jewelry, and other tangible assets don't usually have a beneficiary designation. In these cases, name the asset, its value, the owner, and what type of asset it is. Below are examples of two types of assets, one with a beneficiary designation and another without.

Asset	Value	Asset Owner	Type	Primary	Contingent
Jim's IRA	$350,000	Jim	IRA or retirement account	Lisa	Janie and Jesse's trust
Our home	$450,000	Jim and Lisa	real estate	None	None

This step is designed to help you identify your accounts, determine where they are located, and review the choices you made when opening those accounts. It always surprises me that many of the people I meet with cannot remember what assets they have. I see it most often with those who have worked with several employers, moved several times, and cannot recall if they contributed to retirement plans or not. Chances are you remember the accounts you own and where they are located but you're not so sure about the exact account types or who you've named as beneficiaries. That's easy to fix.

Step 2

Get in touch with your attorney and ask for the specific language recommended to title accounts and to use for beneficiary designations. Some assets will be held in your name, others in joint name with your spouse or partner, and others in the name of a trust (especially if you live in a state with high probate taxes and costs). Your attorney should be willing to review your list and help you identify any necessary changes. Their work really isn't done until you've made changes to all of your accounts and assets that name beneficiaries.

Step 3

Call or email your financial adviser or review your accounts online to find the forms needed to change beneficiary designations using the language provided by the attorney. This is the crucial step. Don't forget to do it or push it off until next week, and then the next and the next and the next. Just do it now.

Step 4

Review. Anytime you update your estate plan, change jobs, or go through a major life event, review the choices you've made and update the forms to reflect any new decisions. The death of a spouse, a divorce, the receipt of an inheritance, your own disability, a significant increase in income or assets, or the sale of a home or purchase of a new one are all great reasons to update your planning and documents. Take the time to conduct this review with a trusted family member or professional team.

The beneficiary form may seem like an afterthought when people start a 401(k) with their employers, apply for life insurance, or set up a Roth IRA. Applications are lengthy, and most of us would rather skip the paperwork. Unfortunately, for families with members who have special needs, this one page of the account form might be the most important. It remains in place for the rest of your life unless you go back and change it, and unless you make sure it's all squared away, that one page can result in a huge headache for your personal representative and loss of benefits for your loved one with a disability.

Use the chart of accounts you put together as a handy checklist and don't dispose of it until you have updated each account and asset.

CHAPTER 11

EMERGENCIES

Earlier, you read about the mother who signed a TOD form for an investment account that named each of her children as recipients of the account upon her passing. One of those children was receiving SSI and Medicaid-funded services, and the money went directly to her instead of transferring to the special-needs trust. A mistake.

Whether it's a misdirected inheritance; gifts given at important life events; an aunt or uncle inclined to offer financial assistance to your son or daughter as a beneficiary on a life insurance policy, a retirement account, or in their will; or lump-sum settlements from insurance companies bequeathed to your family member, benefits can be negatively affected if you're not careful.

Whatever the case, there are several things you can do to fix problems that lead to your family member with special needs receiving countable resources above $2,000.

Spend the Money

The first and easiest option is to spend the money. Find simple or creative ways to get the money out of your family member's name by buying something. Smaller amounts can be spent quickly on purchases like clothes, computers, furniture, and other personal items. If your family member drives, he can own a car. If he does not drive but requires a specialized vehicle driven by someone else, that's also an option. Look into upgrading medical and assistive devices. Booking a travel excursion using the money counts as long as the funds are used for the person with a disability and not for other family members.

One seemingly obvious solution is to give the money to another family member or friend. The money moves out of the person with a disability's account to someone who wants to care for him. Problem solved. Unfortunately, this great idea does not work. Gifting resources to another person is not an option under current Medicaid rules—the money has to benefit the person with special needs who's received the funds. If the gift has strings attached, it's like no gift has been made. If it truly is a gift, then it is not for the benefit of the person with a disability.

Spending to reduce assets so they're below the resource limit of $2,000 preserves benefits. Though it's supposed to be done in the month the funds are received, there are relief measures that can stretch that period by a few months.

Quickly buying necessary items solves the short-term resource problem, but it does not help preserve assets to use for future spending. Ideally, some inheritance money is should be saved for future expenses. After all, computers, furniture, cell phones, and clothes don't last forever.

A common recommendation I've heard from estate-planning attorneys for spending larger amounts quickly is to use those funds to purchase a house or apartment, which is a great idea as it solves two problems—

providing shelter and investing for growth. And yet, while doing so can help you spend larger inheritances, there are some drawbacks. The person with special needs has to live in the house or apartment, yet many of these adults cannot live without ongoing support. Real estate has to be managed—there are maintenance costs, repairs, and taxes to pay.

If someone already owns real estate and has a mortgage, these funds can be used to reduce or pay off the mortgage.

Other Types of Trusts

Another option is to fund a different type of qualifying trust. There are three types of special-needs trusts: third-party funded, first-party funded, and pooled-income.

The first part of this book is designed to help you move quickly to get your estate plan in place. If you plan effectively, the assets for your family member with special needs will go to a third-party-funded special-needs trust. Your money, house, artwork, and other assets go to this type of trust, and your son or daughter does not ever own any of it. It goes to the trust. For you Monopoly fans, it's the card that says "Go directly to Jail. Do not pass Go. Do not collect [any money]."

In any special-needs trust, there are two people to think about—the one giving the money and the one benefitting from it.

Third-party special-needs trusts are funded by someone other than the beneficiary. In my case, I am the third party to my daughter. When I die, part of my assets will be directed to a special-needs trust to benefit her. She will not receive money directly; it goes to the trust, bypassing my daughter. The same is true for you if you structure your estate plan to fund a trust to benefit your family member with a disability.

In <u>first-party</u>-funded special-needs trusts and pooled-income trusts, the <u>funder</u> of the trust and the beneficiary are the same person.

Settlements from insurance cases usually go to a <u>first-party</u>-funded trust. While some people are born with conditions like autism, Down syndrome, or cerebral palsy, others become intellectually and physically disabled as a result of injury. Automobile accidents, institutional neglect, medical harm, falls down flights of stairs and other accidents sometimes can result in a person having a qualifying disability. There's no shortage of personal-injury attorneys seeking monetary compensation, and it's quite possible for a person to receive an award from the court that causes a loss of benefits.

In these cases, an informed attorney will work to direct settlement funds to a first-party special-needs trust. The money technically goes to the disabled individual, who then directs the assets to the <u>first-party</u>-funded trust. Unfortunately, the process isn't as simple as it sounds.

In most states, first-party trusts must be approved before any funds can be transferred to them. The language must be specific and include the potential to reimburse the state should any funds remain. A first-party trust should not be used to make up for a lack of good estate planning—it's an option if something goes wrong but is not ideal. In my state, the approval process is supposed to take less than ninety days, but more often than not, it stretches into six months or more.

The pooled-income trust is similar to the first-party trust. Instead of drafting a new trust for each person who needs one, a pooled income trust is an existing trust that accepts money from multiple beneficiaries who "pool" their money into one trust. Most states have several pooled-income trusts, and these trusts are usually sponsored by nonprofit organizations. Pooled-income-trust accounts are easier to establish than <u>first-party</u>-funded trusts because the basic, underlying fund agreement has been preapproved by the state, and all it takes for a person to start is to fill out a several-page joinder agreement.

Some families prefer the pooled-income trust for the speed with which they can get funds moved and for the immediate appointment of a trustee and investment manager. This type of fund is also useful for people who don't use an investment adviser and don't know where to turn to find a trustee; the sponsor of the pooled-income trust handles those functions.

A significant difference between the three special-needs trusts has to do with where any remainder funds go. When the primary beneficiary in a third-party-funded trust dies, any remaining assets go to the other beneficiaries chosen by those who put the trust in place. For you, this means you can choose other family members as the remainder beneficiaries and keep the assets in the family.

In a first-party trust, Medicaid gets paid back. If any money remains in the trust when the beneficiary dies, the state gets reimbursed up to the amount it paid to support your family member. It cannot claim more than what is in the trust, but it can claim 100 percent of the assets up to how much they spent. Anything left can go to the contingent beneficiaries you've chosen.

In a pooled-income trust, the state loses its right to reclaim trust assets. Those assets stay in the pooled-income trust and can be used to support other beneficiaries.

The decision to use a first-party or pooled-income trust depends on several factors. If you expect there to be assets in the trust after both the beneficiary dies and the state is repaid, then a first-party trust is a better fit. It works better if you want to appoint a trustee who knows your family and can provide both competent and caring service.

If you want speed and simplicity and you prefer that any remainder assets go to help others with qualifying disabilities, the pooled-trust is the way to go. These are better for people who do not have a financial team to assist them with managing assets and making distributions.

There are circumstances where adults with qualifying disabilities benefit from all three types of trusts.

ABLE Accounts

Congress passed legislation in 2014 allowing qualifying adults to hold their own money in a new type of account. With an ABLE account, a person with a disability can, for the first time, have more than $2,000 she can access without being disqualified. These accounts do have rules and limitations; be sure to work with your advisory team to learn more.

ABLE accounts have limited use in estate planning as there is a cap on the dollar amount of contributions that can be made in any calendar year. The cap matches the IRS gift-tax exclusion amount, which is currently $15,000. These accounts work great for smaller estates in combination with spending funds for immediate needs.

ABLE accounts can be used for people receiving inheritances of less than $15,000 as a way to preserve rather than spend those inheritances. An account is opened, and the inheritance goes to the ABLE, where the money can be spent as needed or invested for the future. For larger estates, a first-party or pooled-income trust will be needed.

Pitcher or Strainer?

Often, planners use the water pitcher metaphor when talking about trust planning. The special-needs trust gets filled with money and assets—investment and bank accounts, retirement-plan distributions, life-insurance proceeds, real estate, household goods, and other property. The trust (the pitcher) then pours those assets out to benefit others.

Bring to mind the image of a water pitcher and then a strainer. The pitcher is open at the top, has a spout near the top, and does not have any other holes or openings. The strainer, on the other hand, is open at the top, and the entire bottom is made up of holes. You want water to run through the strainer quickly.

Why this comparison? Good planning seeks to fill the pitcher and then pour it out as needed, but sometimes the contents of the pitcher leak through a small hole. These holes are almost always avoidable. We don't take out a pitcher expecting to find a hole; we fill it trusting that it will work and we can transport water from the kitchen sink to the dining-room table.

It's the same with good planning. It starts with faith and the expectation that by taking the right steps, the planning will go well. In special-needs planning, the small holes are emergencies caused by a lack of action to create a trust, failure to update beneficiary designations, and poor communication.

These small holes are almost always fixable, although the repairs come with great expense of time and money and the process takes away from enjoying life. Don't find yourself worrying about the holes. Focus instead on getting the best pitcher possible for you and your family.

CHAPTER 12

BLUEPRINTS AND THE BUILDING BLOCKS

Your estate plan and special-needs trust are critical to ensuring that each member of your family lives a fulfilling, enjoyable life. Establishing your estate plan preserves valuable benefits, identifies people to take care of your loved ones who are minors or have disabilities, and appoints trusted people to assist with important medical, financial, and legal decisions, if needed.

This book, *30 Days to Your Special Needs Trust*, is designed to help you understand the importance of the special-needs trust and prepare you to hire an attorney and finalize your estate plan quickly. There's no reason to delay; you leave your family at risk by waiting, and it is unlikely the decisions you make today will be much different than they would be in a few months or longer.

But there's more work to do. Your estate plan is the foundational element of a special-needs plan. It is there to protect benefits and appoint people to help in the event of your own death or disability. When this is done, take a deep breath, celebrate and then get ready for more.

It's time to attain financial freedom and the peace of mind that comes with knowing you are building a strong financial life.

The Blueprints method for special-needs planning follows the metaphor of building a house, and the process is the cornerstone of my books and work. No one simply starts building a house. Much thought, planning, and design occurs before any construction starts. There are many decisions made in the planning stage. Will the house have one floor or two? Will it be in town or in the country? And will it be modern or historic? These are just a few examples of the decisions that will need to be made. Paint color, room size, furnishings, tile or wood floors, and hundreds of other decisions follow.

The metaphor makes sense to most people as planning for your future is a complex and time-consuming task. Financial considerations, such as saving for retirement, funding a trust, getting out of debt, building an emergency fund, and having funds to pay for an exciting and fulfilling life require patience, planning, and commitment. There are many steps to the process, steps which must often be taken at the same time.

Financial freedom does not happen overnight. As with the construction of a house, it often seems there is a lot of activity for a long time with little result. Then, all of a sudden, there is shape, color, and something incredible emerges. In financial terms, that something incredible looks like money in the bank, investments in retirement accounts, a plan to fund a trust, and freedom from debt. It can take months to years to feel any progress, but then the moment comes when it all starts fitting together and you and your family start to feel optimistic and secure.

My book, *Financial Freedom for Special Needs Families—9 Building Blocks to Reduce Stress, Preserve Benefits, and Create a Fulfilling Future,* presents these Building Blocks in a specific order. It starts with the dream—What is it you want out of life?—and ends with funding a trust. Each chapter takes you through one of the nine Building Blocks:

1. Dreaming about Your Future

2. Starting to Design

3. Taking Stock

4. Building a Foundation—The Special-Needs Trust

5. Eliminating Debt Forever

6. Financial Stability

7. Protect Your Family

8. Investing for Your Future

9. Funding the Trust

Each Building Block includes worksheets to help you with brainstorming and decision-making. The first four can be finished in a matter of weeks. These are the planning decisions and the foundational elements you'll need to move toward financial freedom. The other five Building Blocks take longer to accomplish, but you will see progress as you pay off debts, build emergency funds, and as the money in your retirement and investment accounts begins to grow.

My book contains worksheets for each chapter to help you leap into action. In fact, you probably have some parts of each Building Block completed, but you may have made a few errors or lack a coherent strategy.

As a whole, the Building Blocks will enable you to live free from the worry that you have not done anything to protect yourself and your family member with special needs. You will feel newfound freedom from stress in your financial life. And once you feel this freedom, you can turn your thoughts and desires to living the most fulfilling life possible. You will be able to put your energy toward enjoying each day, looking forward to the future, and feeling confident that life for your family member with an intellectual or developmental disability will be rewarding, fulfilling, and joyful.

To find out more, please visit my website, **www.robwrubel.com**, or search Rob Wrubel at online booksellers or request copies through local bookstores and libraries.

CHAPTER 13

READY. SET. GO!

My seventeen-year-old daughter with Down syndrome runs track at her high school. As mentioned earlier, each of her races starts with the same process. The runners wait in the holding area until they are called by the officials to the track, where the athletes load into the starting blocks. The starter holds the pistol, counts, then pulls the trigger, and the sprinters fly.

Ready. Set. Go.

As adults, we complicate life, overthink our next steps, hold ourselves back, and wait until the timing is perfect before we act. We justify our procrastination: "I need to know more." "It's too expensive." "I'm too busy right now."

As kids, we just went. Ready. Set. Go. We didn't spend a whole lot of time thinking about the grass being too tall, that we might skin our knees, or that the wind was coming from the wrong direction. We'd just go.

Take that same attitude with your estate planning and special-needs trust. Get moving and get it in place quickly. You'll gain freedom and peace of mind knowing that you've put an important planning building block in place to protect valuable financial and supportive benefits. More likely than not, you will wind up with your estate plan in place; why not start now?

You've heard some popular phrases: *Financial freedom. Peace of mind. Quality of life. Don't worry, be happy. Fear not, want not.* You can live the kind of life these phrases describe, but you won't live it without doing something different from what you're doing now.

One of my clients didn't start planning until she was in her late seventies. Somehow she found out about my workshops. She got out of her house, where she lived with two sons with intellectual and developmental disabilities, and drove twenty minutes to sit in a room full of strangers with a speaker she didn't know. She took a major step by coming to the event. It helped her move forward and by the end of that night she was in contact with an organization that could help her get her sons qualified for benefits as she started to work on her plan.

Before she started this process, she was afraid she'd pass away in her sleep and her sons would be left alone, uncared for and without hope. Now she has a plan in place. She's in touch with several nonprofits that will help her when she needs them. There's funding in place, and her remaining assets will go to a trust to maintain her sons' quality of life.

This mom sleeps better at night. She simplified her financial life and made it easier for someone to step in to pay her bills and transfer her assets. Her estate plan protects benefits, names a successor guardian, and has an appointed trustee. She's engaged nonprofits to step in as her health fails or if there's an emergency.

She could have done all this five, ten, or twenty years earlier and felt more comfortable with less stress about her sons' care. She did not know her options back then, but she acted once she understood her choices and how they'd benefit her family.

As parents of individuals with intellectual and development disabilities, we have different duties than typical parents. Parents of individuals with intellectual and development disabilities must provide more support as our children age. We expect our children to live with us longer. We will fund a trust to pay expenses for family members who do not have as many opportunities.

We also get to experience life differently. I've met countless families who've expressed how much they've learned about themselves, about life, and about other people as a result of their family member with differences. They've told me that they are better people, that they are more caring, and that they've acquired valuable life, personal, and technical skills.

My goal in creating Blueprints—in writing, speaking, and working with families—is to help people live the highest quality of life, for life, for each family member. Families who engage in financial and legal planning find that their stress is reduced and that they can focus on designing and living the life they choose.

Take the next step. Identify beneficiaries, trustees, guardians, and people to fill the other critical roles. Do it quickly. Work with competent people. And then return to making the most of each day.

WORKSHEETS

Chapter 3: Commitment Dates Worksheet

Commitment Date

_____

First Attorney Meeting Date

_____

Chapter 4: Beneficiaries Worksheet

Primary Beneficiaries

Name: _____   Age (if known): _____

Percentage: _____

Name: _____   Age (if known): _____

Percentage: _____

Name: _____   Age (if known): _____

Percentage: _____

Name: _____   Age (if known): _____

Percentage: _____

Contingent Beneficiaries

Name: _____   Age (if known): _____

Percentage: _____

Name: _____   Age (if known): _____

Percentage: _____

Name: _____   Age (if known): _____

Percentage: _____

Name: _____   Age (if known):_____

Percentage: _____

Chapter 5: Trustee Worksheet

Primary Trustee

Name: _____

Successor Trustees (or Potential Candidates)

Name: _____

Name: _____

Name: _____

Name: _____

Name: _____

Chapter 6: Guardian Worksheet

Primary Guardian

Name: _____

Successor Guardians (or Potential Candidates)

Name: _____

Name: _____

Name: _____

Name: _____

Name: _____

Chapter 6: Personal Representative Worksheet

Primary Personal Representative

Name: _____

Successor Personal Representatives (or Potential Candidates)

Name: _____

Name: _____

Name: _____

Name: _____

Name: _____

Chapter 6: General POA Worksheet

Primary General Power of Attorney (POA)

Name: _____

Successor General Power of Attorney (or Potential Candidates)

Name: _____

Name: _____

Name: _____

Name: _____

Name: _____

Chapter 6: Medical POA Worksheet

Primary Medical Power of Attorney (POA)

Name: _____

Successor Medical Power of Attorney (or Potential Candidates)

Name: _____

Name: _____

Name: _____

Name: _____

Name: _____

Chapter 7: Choosing an Attorney

Names of Attorneys to Interview

Name: _____

Name: _____

Name: _____

Sample Questions

1. What is your experience working with families like mine?

2. How many third-party trusts do you write in a typical year?

3. How many first-party funded trusts do you write in a typical year?

4. Tell me about your continuing education in this area.

5. How do you charge? Flat fee or hourly?

6. What states are you licensed to practice in?

7. How long have you been an estate-planning attorney?

8. Can you provide references of recent clients?

Chapter 8: Getting Organized Checklist

☐ Bank or credit-union account statements

☐ Investment account statements

☐ Individual retirement accounts and employer retirement account statements, including 401(k) and 403(b) accounts

☐ Pension estimates and values

☐ Annuity statements

☐ Life-insurance policy information (coverage summary pages, recent statement, and/or last invoices)

☐ Real-estate current values (include estimate of purchase dates)

☐ Mortgage information—include current balance, interest rate, payment amount, number of years, and start date

☐ Credit card statements

☐ Student loan statements

☐ Homeowner's insurance and car insurance policy declaration pages

☐ List of significant personal property, such as automobiles, boats, and jewelry

☐ Disability-insurance policy page and last invoice

☐ Long-term care insurance policy page and last invoice

☐ Buy/sell agreements

- ☐ Business valuations

- ☐ Stock option plan information

- ☐ Deferred compensation contracts

- ☐ Social Security statement

- ☐ Collectibles information, such as coins, art and antiques, and estimated values

- ☐ Other

A Word on Language

This book and the other parts of the Blueprints series strive to use person-centered language. There is no "Down syndrome person." There are only people with Down syndrome. My daughter, your family members, and all the wonderful people with disabilities we meet are people first and are not defined by their labels. There are many times where I used the words "Special-Needs Families" and "Special-Needs Trusts." Part of this is so that you are familiar with the language your attorney, CPA, and financial planner will use. The other part has to do with my desire for a language economy that makes this book easier to read. There are many times where sentences would be too long or too confusing if I used "a family with a member who has an intellectual or developmental disability" instead of "special-needs person." When I talk about a specific person, I use people-centered language. When referring to families, trusts, or planning, I use the term "special-needs."

Acknowledgments

There are many people to thank as this book would not be finished and published without their help, encouragement, and support.

Most of this book was written as the 2020 Covid-19 pandemic swept across the world. My family and I spent many days together, and somehow enjoyed those days by getting outside to play soccer and baseball, singing songs in the kitchen, and cooking all kinds of treats. We had chocolate cake, chocolate chip cookies, crumb cake, apple pie, and the tour de force—a New Orleans food day, complete with homemade beignets, shrimp po' boy sandwiches, and jambalaya.

My family is incredible: fun to be with, busy with their lives, and as proud of me as I am of them (which is a ton.) Thank you, Benjie, Sarah, and Annie. I love you all, and I love watching you grow, develop, and turn into wonderful people. Kelly Smith's patience, compassion, and love keep me moving forward, and I appreciate her being with me. My parents, Myra and Charlie, are supportive and have given me the education and work ethic that shapes me daily, and my brothers, Julian and Bill, are helpful in their encouragement and support.

Jerry Dorris came through with another spectacular book cover that mixes the seriousness of the topic with celebrations of people with disabilities. The team at Eschler Editing, including Kathy Jenkins and Michele Preisendorf, offered excellent editing services and fantastic advice with their comments and suggestions. Deana Riddle took my basic document and turned it into a readable, interesting looking book with her eye for design. I appreciate her flexibility in working with me as different pieces came to her over time. Her knowledge of publishing platforms helped take this book you hold from digital files to the finished product you hold in your hands.

Martha Bullen coached me through the final phases of publishing. Her experience is vast and her guidance remarkable. She supported me in writing this book by keeping me on track to get my work from a draft to a completed and final version.

It's largely because of the people I work with at Cascade Investment Group that I am able to continue offering excellent advice and service to my clients while I write, publish, and speak with families who have members with special needs. Scott Rethi, particularly, keeps me on track, reads my drafts, and arranges for my speaking to groups.

Starr Hall has been a phenomenon in helping me reach more people than I ever imagined and she brought to my team incredible people. Tiffany Windsor, Gen Herres and Donald Tremblay have all helped get the message of the work I do in front of media, families and other professionals.

I cannot say enough about the kindness and compassion of Eric Stonestreet, Joe Mantegna and Jack Canfield. Each holds a special place in my heart for his ability to reach people, encourage families and lead with thoughtfulness and empathy.

My daughter, Sarah, is a varsity cheerleader at her high school, runs track, and spends much of her school time in a typical classroom. Thank you to everyone who makes it possible for her to enjoy school and to learn and be included in the many activities and worthwhile pursuits that go on there. She thrives in an environment of support and inclusion and my hope is that all schools make the effort that hers does.

ABOUT THE AUTHOR

Rob Wrubel, CFP° AIF° AEP°, is the award-winning, best-selling author of *Financial Freedom for Special-Needs Families, Protect Your Family* and the creator of Blueprints, a financial-planning process designed to help families with a special-needs member get out of debt, save for retirement, and protect and enhance potential government benefits for their family member with special needs. Rob is a senior vice president with Cascade Investment Group, Inc., in Colorado Springs, Colorado.

Rob has three children. In 2003, his middle child was born with Down syndrome. A few months after her birth, Rob began researching how financial planning for a family with a member who has special needs is different from planning for a typical family. He has focused his practice on working with families who fit this description and the professionals and organizations that serve them.

He donates his time through his direct support of several organizations. He served as a board member and investment committee chair of the Pikes Peak Community Foundation and as president of the Cheyenne Village Board of Directors and CASA of the Pikes Peak Region. He has also served on the board of directors of the Ronald McDonald House Charities of Southern Colorado, the Colorado Fund for People with Disabilities, and the Colorado Springs Down Syndrome Association.

Rob and his family live in Colorado. He is a graduate of Wesleyan University in Middletown, Connecticut.